THE TOTAL RIDER

HEALTH & FITNESS FOR THE EQUESTRIAN

Tom Holmes

The Total Rider
Health & Fitness for the Equestrian

Published in the United States of America by
Half Halt Press, Inc.
P.O. Box 67
Boonsboro, MD 21713

Cover design by Graphics Plus, Inc.
Text illustrations by Susan Wood
Inside text design by Gallagher Wood Design

Holmes, Tom, 1959–
      The total rider : health & fitness for the equestrian / Tom
   Holmes.
          p.   cm.
      Includes bibliographical references.
      ISBN 0–939481–44–8
      1. Horsemanship– –Physiological aspects.   2. Horsemen and
   horsewomen– –Health and hygiene.   3. Physical fitness.   I. Title.
   RC1220.H67H65   1995
   613. 7′08′8798– –dc20   95–45069
                                                                CIP

TABLE OF CONTENTS

Accept your role as an athlete and realize the benefits

of a finely tuned body and mind.

Enjoy life and competition in good health.

Tom Holmes

INTRODUCTION

What does it take to be a successful competitive rider? Most experts agree it is a combination of desire, determination, focus, balance, flexibility, muscle awareness, and muscular endurance, to list a few. Obviously, it's not necessary to have the phenomenal talents of an NBA All-Star basketball player to be a great rider, but equestrian success does require finely tuned physical and mental abilities.

Traditionally, riding skills have been developed through long hours of training in the saddle, a 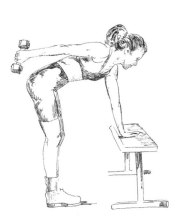 proven formula for which there is no viable substitute. This fact still remains true: If you want to be a successful rider, you must train hard and intelligently in the saddle . . . This is the foundation upon which winning is built. However, intensive riding is not all you can do to become a better rider.

By improving your physical and mental fitness you can utilize more of your full athletic potential to further develop your riding skills and competitiveness. A comprehensive fitness program can enhance your existing riding abilities. Achieving a higher degree of fitness will make your reactions quicker and your cues more precise. It will improve your balance, flexibility, and muscular endurance. By expanding your athletic potential you will ride with new confidence and authority.

The Total Rider combines exercise, health, and nutrition principles into a balanced and integrated fitness program designed to compliment your riding program. It is the result of a  cooperative effort utilizing the expertise of health and fitness specialist and equestrian Barbara J. Beck, Ph.D., exercise physiologist Kay Roth, Ph.D., nutrition extension specialist Jennifer Anderson Ph.D., R.D., renowned equine-sports psychologist Dr. Margot Nacey, numerous exercise professionals, and world class equestrians (see *Acknowledgments*, page 121). A cross-section of highly respected trainers and riders throughout the United States were studied and certain physical and mental qualities were found to be essential in developing the "ideal" rider in each of the following riding disciplines: dressage, hunt seat, cross-country and stadium jumping, reining, gymkhana, saddleseat, sidesaddle, and english and western pleasure. A blend of new and traditional exercises was then formulated to enhance these positive qualities. Finally, the fitness workout was integrated with practical health and

nutritional guidelines to maximize your fitness benefits, and a mental practice program to help you get the most out of your skills. All of the physical and mental exercises in **The Total Rider** are intended to supplement your current riding program, and can be performed in the home, gym, or barn. **The Total Rider** is divided into three parts:

■ The *Equestrian Workout* targets your balance, flexibility, posture, muscular endurance, strength, and muscle awareness. These attributes are instrumental in developing a successful seat for riding regardless of your style.

■ The *Nutrition Strategy*, latest in nutrition information will help you formulate a healthy diet that will increase and stabilize your energy levels throughout the day. With the right nutrition strategy, you will fatigue less easily, maintain mental sharpness, and combined with consistent exercise, lower your body fat percentage.

■ In *The Mental Advantage* proven mental relaxation, stress management, focusing, and visualization techniques developed by psychologist Dr. Margot Nacey will put you on top of your mental game.

■ Incorporated into *The Equestrian Workout* and *The Mental Advantage* Program are relaxation

techniques useful in relieving muscular tension associated with stress and injury.

It's important to note that the key to success in any exercise program is not the type of equipment you use, but the mental attitude and approach you maintain. Simply put, you must train smart in order to train successfully. So, before you begin your workout, let's discuss some important fitness principles that will guide you to a new level of health and fitness:

■ First, you should receive a complete physical checkup from your physician before you begin any exercise program.

■ Second, let's debunk the most common of all exercise myths: "No pain, no gain." This rule applies only to an elite class of athletes whose highly conditioned bodies are capable of pushing past the normal physical limits intended for the rest of us mortals. Unless you're a world class marathon runner or Arnold Schwarzeneggar's heir apparent, the rule of thumb for you should be: If you feel pain.. . . Stop! This refers specifically to a

sharp, shooting pain, not the mild aching sensation you will experience during exercise as your muscles begin to tire. Many people learn to enjoy this tired sensation as it leaves a nice, warm feeling in your muscles, elevates your spirits, and is your body's way of communicating that you are working hard enough.

Your body is amazingly accurate in informing you of its needs. The problem is that most people don't know how to listen to their body and train instinctively. If your shoulders are overworked, then rest them that day and exercise other areas of you body. If you feel that certain muscles are already highly developed, then concentrate more on weaker muscles, so you can ultimately achieve a balanced level of conditioning throughout your body.

■ For any fitness program to be fully productive, you must combine three factors:

Exercise + Nutrition + Rest

It is this combination that will enable you to gain the most from your efforts by increasing the efficiency and quality of your exercises. Proper nutrition gives your muscle cells the nutrients they need to sustain exercise, and to recover and grow. Rest is critical for your

muscles to have time to recover before you stress them again in your next workout, thus keeping the quality of each workout high and promoting maximum toning. You do not have to rest from your daily riding routine to compensate for added exercise. A good rule of thumb for insuring adequate rest is 48 hours between strenuous workouts. It is also wise to take a full week off from heavy exercise every 8 to 10 weeks to thoroughly rest your body and to prevent overtraining.

■ Perhaps the most effective method to increase the quality of your exercise is to maximize every repetition by mentally focusing on the primary muscle as it is being worked. Concentrate on the sensation in the muscle as it contracts and extends, and maintain continuous tension in a slow and deliberate manner throughout the entire range of motion. This requires good form and slow, smooth movements. The idea is not to do as many repetitions as you can, but to make your muscles work as hard as possible in each individual rep. In the end, you will complete fewer reps, but you will produce better results, and maximizing results is your primary goal in any exercise program, not merely counting repetitions or minutes.

■ Always attempt to use good form and keep your movements smooth and deliberate; never jerk or bounce as this is very inefficient and may lead to injury.

- Drink plenty of water during and after exercise. This prevents dehydration, and assists in flushing toxins/wastes produced by your muscle cells during exercise out of your body.

- Vary your exercise routine to avoid boredom. You don't have to change the entire program, one or two exercises is sufficient to keep you fresh and looking forward to your next workout.

- Loosen up and have fun with your fitness program. Take a bike ride, go swimming or cross-country skiing, or devise a game at home or at the barn. Turn on

the stereo and work out with your spouse or several friends. You'll have more fun, and you'll discover a wonderful new source of motivation. Fitness should not only increase your riding skills and your capacity to enjoy life, but should be enjoyable itself.

- Exercising will improve your muscle awareness, which will enable you to be more precise and knowledgeable in your movements in the saddle.

- Remember that the exercises in *The Equestrian Workout* section are designed to enhance your current riding program and are not a substitute for training in the saddle.

10 REASONS TO EXERCISE

1. **Exercise improves the quality of your life.**
   The old adage, "Add life to your years, as well as years to your life by exercise" has considerable merit. A properly designed exercise program will give you more energy to do the activities you enjoy.

2. **Exercise relieves depression.**
   In her book, Mental Skills for Physical People, Dr. Dorothy V. Harris concluded that, "exercise is nature's best tranquilizer." Researchers have found, for example, that mildly to moderately depressed individuals who engage in aerobic exercise 15-30 minutes a day at least every other day typically experience a positive mood swing in two to three weeks.

3. **Exercise prevents certain types of cancer.**
   Studies have found that men and women who exercise are less likely to get colon cancer. Research has also suggested that women who do not exercise have more than two and one half times the risk of developing cancer of the reproductive system and almost twice the chance of getting breast cancer.

4. **Exercise enhances your self-image.**
   Research has documented the assertion that individuals who exercise regularly feel better about themselves than sedentary individuals.

5. **Exercise relieves stress and anxiety.**
   Exercise dissipates those hormones and other chemicals which build up during periods of high stress. Exercise also generates a period of substantial emotional and physical relaxation that sets in approximately an hour and a half after an intense workout.

6. **Exercise reduces the risk of heart disease.**
   Experts have found that non-exercisers have twice the risk of developing heart disease than individuals who exercise regularly.

7. **Exercise slows the aging process.**
   Proper exercise can increase your aerobic capacity as you get older, instead of losing aerobic fitness, as older people often do at the typical rate of ten percent per year. Past the age of thirty, you can actually become more aerobically fit if you exercise. Exercise can also result in better skin tone and muscle tone.

8. **Exercise increases the good (HDL) cholesterol.**
   Exercise is one of the few voluntary activities that is effective in raising your level of HDL— the type of cholesterol that lowers your risk of heart disease.

9. **Exercise improves the quality of sleep.**
   Researchers have found that exercisers go to sleep more quickly, sleep more soundly and are more refreshed than individuals who do not exercise.

10. **Exercise improves mental sharpness.**
    Numerous studies have shown that individuals who exercise regularly have better memories, better reaction times, and better concentration than nonexercisers.

    Reprinted from the Stairmaster Wellness Newsletter, Vol. 1, Iss. 1; written by Dr. James A. Peterson and Dr. Cedric X. Bryant; used by permission of Stairmaster Sports/Medical Products, Inc.

THE
EQUESTRIAN
WORKOUT

INTRODUCTION

The exercises in *The Equestrian Workout* section are divided into three types to give you a more effective workout:

Warm-up. It should be performed **before** stretching, working out, or riding.

Type 1 exercises are comprised of strength and muscular endurance exercises, good hands exercises, and seat specific exercises. These exercises should be performed **3 times a week.** (See *Superset* instructions on page 18.)

Type 2 exercises are comprised of 12 flexibility-posture exercises and 2 balance exercises. These exercises should be performed **every day** for full benefit. Only by stretching daily will you see any significant improvement in flexibility. You can also use the flexibility-posture exercises to stretch out before riding.

A suggested weekly workout schedule is given in the box below.

Beginner, universal, intermediate, and advanced exercises are provided so you choose the right exercises for your fitness level. Look to the title bar at the top of each page for that exercise's level of difficulty.

Beginner exercises are designed for the individual starting a fitness program for the first time, or resuming one after a prolonged period of reduced activity. **All readers (regardless of fitness level) should start with the beginner exercises, then progress slowly to the more challenging levels.**

Universal exercises are for individuals of all fitness levels. The difficulty level of these exercises may be raised by increasing the number of repetitions or by adding weight.

Intermediate exercises are for the individual who has comfortably completed the beginner level exercises and is ready for a higher degree of difficulty.

Advanced exercises are for the individual who has comfortably completed the intermediate level exercises and is ready for a greater challenge.

Alternate exercises have been included to provide a little variety to help you stay motivated.

A weekly workout schedule may look like this:			
Monday	warm-up +	workout	(30, 45, or 60 minutes)
Tuesday	warm-up +	stretching-posture-balance	(type 2)
Wednesday	warm-up +	workout	(30, 45, or 60 minutes)
Thursday	warm-up +	stretching-posture-balance	(type 2)
Friday	warm-up +	workout	(30, 45, or 60 minutes)
Saturday	warm-up +	stretching-posture-balance	(type 2)
Sunday	warm-up +	stretching-posture-balance	(type 2)

- Each alternate exercise is found on the page immediately after the exercise it is intended to replace.

- Exercise is only as effective as you make it. You can experience substantial benefits from your workout if you exercise intelligently and stay motivated, focused, and precise in form. Here are some helpful tips on exercising wisely:

- Perform each exercise in a smooth and controlled manner. Quick, jerky movements decrease the efficiency of the exercise and often lead to injury.

- Exercise requires mental concentration. Read your instructions carefully and focus on your form during every single repetition. Precise form creates maximum efficiency and pays off with superior results.

- Move quickly between each exercise (30-60 seconds). However, it's OK if you need to take more time and rest.

- You should be well hydrated before you begin any workout and should take small sips of water during your workout to stay hydrated and to stabilize your energy level. Don't wait until you are noticeably thirsty, by then your energy level has already dropped.

- Exercise with a partner, if possible. A good exercise partner will provide support, motivation, help you monitor your form, and enable you to get more oomph out of your workout.

- For many people, time constraints are a real problem. If you don't have the time to perform the entire exercise program . . . do what you can. Each exercise, if done well, will help improve your fitness level and riding skill.

- **Exercise can be enjoyable and rewarding, so have some fun with it!**

30 MINUTE WORKOUT

Adequate time is not always available. So, for those days when time is short, try this 30 minute workout. You will get a good basic workout on your most important riding muscles.

30 MINUTE WORKOUT					
BEGINNER		**INTERMEDIATE**		**ADVANCED**	
Warm-up		**Warm-up**		**Warm-up**	
Crunches	p. 20	Crunches	p. 21	Crunches	p. 22, 23
Oblique Curl	p. 35	Oblique Curl	p. 36	Oblique Curl	p. 37
The Pointer	p. 25	Chest Lift	p. 26	The Advanced Pointer	p. 27
The Seated Fly	p. 38	The Seated Fly	p. 38	The Seated Fly	p. 38
Adductor Lift	p. 28	Adductor Lift	p. 28	Adductor Lift	p. 28
The Squeeze	p. 30	The Squeeze	p. 30	The Squeeze	p. 30
Steeple	p. 50	Steeple	p. 50	Steeple	p. 50
Angry Cat &		Angry Cat &		Angry Cat &	
Sway-back Horse	p. 63	Sway-back Horse	p. 63	Sway-back Horse	p. 63
Hip Stretch	p. 64	Hip Stretch	p. 64	Hip Stretch	p. 64
Starter's Stretch	p. 65	Starter's Stretch	p. 65	Starter's Stretch	p. 65
Sumo Stretch	p. 69	Sumo Stretch	p. 69	Sumo Stretch	p. 69
Push-the-Wall-Down	p. 71	Push-the-Wall-Down	p. 71	Push-the-Wall-Down	p. 71
Soleus Stretch	p. 72	Soleus Stretch	p. 72	Soleus Stretch	p. 72

You can customize your workout by adding any exercises that address your personal needs and weaknesses.

45 MINUTE WORKOUT

When you have a little more time on your hands, try this 45 minute workout. You can customize your workout to fit your needs by including additional exercises that address your personal weaknesses.

45 MINUTE WORKOUT					
BEGINNER		**INTERMEDIATE**		**ADVANCED**	
Warm-up		**Warm-up**		**Warm-up**	
Crunches	p. 20	Crunches	p. 21	Crunches	p. 22,23
Oblique Curl	p. 35	Oblique Curl	p. 36	Oblique Curl	p. 37
The Pointer	p. 25	Chest Lift	p. 26	The Advanced Pointer	p. 27
The Seated Fly	p. 38	The Seated Fly	p. 38	The Seated Fly	p. 38
Adductor Lift	p. 28	Adductor Lift	p. 28	Adductor Lift	p. 28
The Squeeze	p. 30	The Squeeze	p. 30	The Squeeze	p. 30
Hamstring Lift	p. 31	Hamstring Lift	p. 31	Hamstring Lift	p. 31
Quad Lift	p. 32	Quad Lift	p. 32	Quad Lift	p. 32
Wall Pushes	p. 40	Kneeling Push-ups	p. 41	Push-ups	p. 42
Forward Arm Raise	p. 43	Forward Arm Raise	p. 43	Forward Arm Raise	p. 43
Steeple	p. 50	Steeple	p. 50	Steeple	p. 50
Dorsal Flex	p. 59	Crosslegged Bow	p. 60	Crosslegged Bow	p. 60
Ventral Stretch	p. 61	Ventral Stretch	p. 62	Ventral Stretch	p. 62
Hip Stretch	p. 64	Hip Stretch	p. 64	Hip Stretch	p. 64
Starter's Stretch	p. 65	Starter's Stretch	p. 65	Starter's Stretch	p. 65
Seated Ham Stretch	p. 66	Seated Ham Stretch	p. 66	Seated Ham Stretch	p. 66
Quad Stretch	p. 68	Quad Stretch	p. 66	Quad Stretch	p. 68
Sumo Stretch	p. 69	Sumo Stretch	p. 69	Sumo Stretch	p. 69
Push-the-Wall-Down	p. 71	Push-the-Wall-Down	p. 71	Push-the-Wall-Down	p. 71
Soleus Stretch	p. 72	Soleus Stretch	p. 72	Soleus Stretch	p. 72
Corner Flex	p. 73	Corner Flex	p. 73	Corner Flex	p. 73
The Stork	p. 76	The Stork	p. 77	The Stork	p. 78

60 MINUTE WORKOUT

The 60 minute workout is for those of you dedicated to reaching your full fitness-riding potential.

60 MINUTE WORKOUT					
BEGINNER Warm-up		**INTERMEDIATE** Warm-up		**ADVANCED** Warm-up	
Crunches	p. 20	Crunches	p. 21	Crunches	p. 22,23
The Pointer	p. 25	Chest Lift	p. 26	The Advanced Pointer	p. 27
Adductor Lift	p. 28	Adductor Lift	p. 28	Adductor Lift	p. 28
The Squeeze	p. 30	The Squeeze	p. 30	The Squeeze	p. 30
Hamstring Lift	p. 31	Hamstring Lift	p. 31	Hamstring Lift	p. 31
Quad Lift	p. 32	Quad Lift	p. 32	Quad Lift	p. 32
Heel Raise	p. 34	Heel Raise	p. 34	Heel Raise	p. 34
Oblique Curl	p. 35	Oblique Curl	p. 36	Oblique Curl	p. 37
The Seated Fly	p. 38	The Seated Fly	p. 38	The Seated Fly	p. 38
Wall Pushes	p. 40	Kneeling Push-ups	p. 40	Push-ups	p. 40
Forward Arm Raise	p. 43	Forward Arm Raise	p. 43	Forward Arm Raise	p. 43
Wrist Swing	p. 44	Wrist Swing	p. 44	Wrist Swing	p. 44
Kick-backs	p. 45	Kick-backs	p. 45	Kick-backs	p. 45
Rotation Curl	p. 47	Rotation Curl	p. 47	Rotation Curl	p. 47
Orange Crush	p. 49	Orange Crush	p. 49	Orange Crush	p. 49
Steeple	p. 50	Steeple	p. 50	Steeple	p. 50
Seat specific exercise	p. 52	Seat specific exercise	p. 52	Seat specific exercise	p. 52
Dorsal Flex	p. 59	Crosslegged Bow	p. 60	Crosslegged Bow	p. 60
Ventral Stretch	p. 61	Ventral Stretch	p. 62	Ventral Stretch	p. 62
Angry Cat &		Angry Cat &		Angry Cat &	
Sway-back Horse	p. 63	Sway-back Horse	p. 63	Sway-back Horse	p. 63
Hip Stretch	p. 64	Hip Stretch	p. 64	Hip Stretch	p. 64
Starter's Stretch	p. 65	Starter's Stretch	p. 65	Starter's Stretch	p. 65
Seated Ham Stretch	p. 66	Seated Ham Stretch	p. 66	Seated Ham Stretch	p. 66
Quad Stretch	p. 68	Quad Stretch	p. 68	Quad Stretch	p. 68
Sumo Stretch	p. 69	Sumo Stretch	p. 69	Sumo Stretch	p. 69
Push-the-Wall-Down	p. 71	Push-the-Wall-Down	p. 71	Push-the-Wall-Down	p. 71
Soleus Stretch	p. 72	Soleus Stretch	p. 72	Soleus Stretch	p. 72
Corner Flex	p. 73	Corner Flex	p. 73	Corner Flex	p. 73
Reach-for-the-Sky	p. 75	Reach-for-the-Sky	p. 75	Reach-for-the-Sky	p. 75
The Stork	p. 76	The Stork	p. 77	The Stork	p. 78
Kneeling Balance Board	p. 83	Kneeling Balance Board	p. 83	Kneeling Balance Board	p. 84

MUSCLE REFERENCE GUIDE

MUSCLES	STRENGTH-MUSCLE ENDURANCE	FLEXIBILITY-POSTURE-BALANCE
Abdominals	Crunches 5-Way Crunches Hard Rocks Oblique Curl	Ventral Stretch
Back	The Pointer Chest Lift The Advanced Pointer Extreme Skier	Dorsal Flex Angry Cat & Sway-back Horse
Upper Back	The Seated Fly	
Hip Extensors	The Pointer The Advanced Pointer Extreme Skier	Hip Stretch Dorsal Flex
Hip Flexors	Crunches 5-Way Crunches	Starter's Stretch
Adductors (inner thigh)	Adductor Lift Adductor Flys	Sumo Stretch Adductor Stretch
Abductors (outer thigh)	Abductor Lift	
Hamstrings	Hamstring Lift	Seated Ham Stretch Standing Ham Stretch
Quadriceps	Quad Lift	Quad Stretch
Gastrocnemius (calves)	Heel Raise	Push-the-Wall-Down
Soleus (calves)	Heel Raise	Soleus Stretch
Chest	Wall Pushes Kneeling Push-ups Push-ups	Corner Flex
Shoulders	Forward Arm Raise	
Biceps	Rotation Curl Hammer Curl	
Triceps	Kick-backs Overhead Extensions	
Wrist Extensors	Wrist Swing	Steeple (for dexterity)
Wrist Flexors	Orange Crush	
Posture specific	Reach-for-the-Sky	
Balance		The Stork Standing Balance Board Kneeling Balance Board

WARM-UP

Always begin with a warm-up

Your workout begins with the gradual warm-up detailed on page 13. Why is a warm-up important? Its purpose is to elevate your deep muscle and over-all body temperatures in preparation for stretching. More specifically, a warm-up will:

- Lessen the potential for injury during conditioning and stretching. When you stretch a cold muscle you risk tearing muscle fibers and their tendinous attachments.

- Reduce muscle soreness.

- Speed up your metabolism and nerve impulse transmissions, and increase your blood flow and oxygen supply . . . all of which result in improved performance and physical working capacity during exercise.

Here are some warm-up guidelines:

- Begin with an easy range of motion and intensity and gradually increase to a moderate range of motion and intensity.

- You are warm enough when you begin to sweat after at least 10 minutes of warm-up.

- No more than 15 minutes should elapse from the end of your warm-up and the beginning of your exercises/activity.

A warm-up can be performed almost anywhere. It can be any moderate activity that sufficiently raises your body temperature (it causes you to sweat). Here are 3 excellent outdoor warm-up activities:

- A moderate-brisk walk for 10 - 15 minutes.

- A moderate bike ride for 10 - 15 minutes.

- Briskly leading your horse for 10 - 15 minutes.

If the weather isn't to your liking or you just don't want to venture outside, this simple, all-weather warm-up will get you primed for your workout:

1. Begin by walking in place with your arms down at your sides. After 1 minute, begin raising your knees higher and slowly swinging your arms front to back in unison with your steps. Start with small movements and gradually increase to larger movements. To add a little variety you may also:

- Raise your arms above your head in time with your steps.

- Extend your arms out to the sides in time with your steps.

- Extend your arms in front of your body in time with your steps.

- Step heel in front and toe in back.

- Dance like a swan singing "Born Free" (individual stylistic interpretation is OK).

2. If you have surpassed 10 minutes and you are sweating, then you have successfully raised your body/muscle temperatures to the desired level. So stop singing and begin your exercising/stretching as soon as possible (within 10 minutes . . . tops).

Type 1: Strength/Muscular Endurance

INTRODUCTION

Your **Type 1** exercises include strength-muscular endurance, good hands, and seat specific exercises.

Supersets

You will superset all of your strength-muscular endurance and good hands exercises. Supersetting means simply that you alternate sets between 2 exercises. For example, you will superset *Crunches* with *The Pointer* :

SUPERSET

Perform **1** set of **Crunches** then **immediately** perform **1** set of **The Pointer**.

Rest for 15 - 60 seconds.

Perform 2nd set of **Crunches** then **immediately** perform 2nd set of **The Pointer**.

You are now finished with both exercises and you can move onto the next.

Strength/Muscular Endurance:

Muscular endurance is your muscle's ability to contract repeatedly against resistance. Any improvement in muscular endurance is closely connected with improvement in strength. As your strength increases so does your muscular endurance. As a rider-athlete you can benefit from this training in several ways:

- It will strengthen your muscles, tendons, ligaments, joint capsules, and even your bones. These will increase in density and become more resistant to injury.

- It will enable you to work/play longer and harder without experiencing debilitating muscle fatigue.

- It will improve your muscle coordination, muscle awareness, and agility helping you become more precise in the saddle and enhancing your riding appearance. Agility is your ability to make a quick and coordinated change in direction. It is crucial to any successful athletic-competitive performance and it can help you avoid potential accident and injury.

- Strength and muscular endurance training will positively enhance your stretching program and your dynamic flexibility.

- These exercises will not dramatically increase your muscle size and density They work primarily to improve the efficiency of your muscle fibers as your strength and muscular endurance increase. Through consistent and correct use of these exercises your muscles will show increased tone and definition.

(Note: Consider this possible scenario. You're in temporary disagreement with your horse, yet due to your improved physical capabilities you're able to gracefully maintain your balance, stylishly retain your composure, and instantly regain your seat. Needless to say, you successfully avoid unscheduled contact with the ground.)

Here are a few guidelines for safe and efficient strength and muscular endurance training:

- Take it slow and easy for the first week if you are performing these exercises for the first time or after a layoff of 2 weeks or more. Avoid unnecessary extreme soreness and allow your body sufficient time to adjust before you raise your intensity level.

■ Expect mild soreness to occur when you begin exercising and any time you increase your intensity. This is OK. You will eventually begin to enjoy this sensation . . . seriously, it could happen.

■ Follow all exercise instructions precisely.

■ Your movements during exercise should be smooth and controlled. Jerking and bouncing movements are very inefficient and can cause injury.

■ Occasionally drink small sips of water during your workout to help avoid dehydration and to help maintain a high energy level.

■ Get the most out of each exercise by focusing on your primary muscles during every single repetition and by making those muscles work as hard as possible . . . this is how you success-fully raise your intensity.

■ Move quickly from one exercise to another. . . 15 - 30 seconds between exercises is recom-mended for the *maximum* fitness benefit. Take more time if needed.

Good Hands

The Good Hands exercises are designed to help you ride with softer and more precise hands by improving the dexterity, muscular endurance, and strength in your fingers and forearms.

Seat Specifics

See pages 52-55. Choose the appropriate exercise for your style of riding: forward seat (hunter, jumper, english pleasure, etc.), balanced seat (dressage, western-gymkhana, etc.), or saddleseat.

CRUNCHES

How important is developing strong abdominal muscles to your overall fitness and to you as an equestrian-athlete?

Answer: Your abdominals are engaged in nearly every movement you make. They enable you to flex forward at the waist, to twist at the waist, to stabilize your "trunk", and to use your arms and legs in independent and coordinated movements. Weak abdominal muscles contribute to poor balance and agility and to the development of chronic lower back problems.

Conclusion: You need all of the abdominal strength you can get . . . so start crunching.

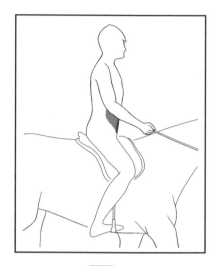

█ **primary muscles**
█

- ❏ Lie on your back with your knees bent and your feet flat on the floor.
- ❏ Place your hands at your sides or between your legs.
- ❏ Position your head as if you are clutching a tennis ball under your chin. This will place your head in a neutral position and reduce the amount of stress on your neck by allowing it to follow the same arching motion as your back.
- ❏ Squeeze your abdominal muscles and slowly curl up toward your knees until your shoulder blades are off the floor.
- ❏ Hold for 1 second.
- ❏ Exhale as you crunch . . . allow your contracting abdominal muscles and diaphragm to push your breath out.
- ❏ Inhaling softly, slowly lower your upper body until your shoulder blades touch the floor to complete 1 repetition.
- ❏ Repeat until you reach fatigue.
- ❏ This will complete 1 set
- ❏ Perform a total of 2 sets.

SUPERSET
30 min. workout: Superset with Oblique Curl (see pg 35).
45 min. workout: Superset with Oblique Curl (see pg 35).
60 min. workout: Superset with The Pointer (see pg 25).

CRUNCHES

INTERMEDIATE

- ❑ Lie on your back with your knees bent and your feet flat on the floor. Fold your hands across your chest.
- ❑ Slowly curl toward your knees until your shoulder blades are off the floor.
- ❑ Exhale as you crunch.
- ❑ Hold for 1 second then lower yourself until your shoulder blades touch the floor.

- ❑ Inhale as you lower.
- ❑ Repeat until fatigue.
- ❑ Perform 2 sets.

SUPERSET
30 min. workout: Superset with Oblique Curl (see pg 36).
45 min. workout: Superset with Oblique Curl (see pg 36).
60 min. workout: Superset with Chest Lift (see pg 26).

CRUNCHES

ADVANCED

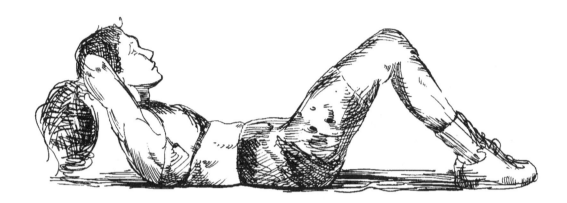

- ❏ Lie on your back with your knees bent and your feet flat on the floor.
- ❏ Clasp your hands behind your neck.
- ❏ Slowly curl toward your knees until your shoulder blades are off the floor. Do not pull your neck up with your arms.
- ❏ Exhale as you crunch.
- ❏ Hold for 1 second then lower yourself until your shoulder blades touch the floor.

- ❏ Inhale as you lower.
- ❏ Repeat until fatigue.
- ❏ Perform 2 sets.

SUPERSET
30 min. workout: Superset with Oblique Curl (see pg 37).
45 min. workout: Superset with Oblique Curl (see pg 37).
60 min. workout: Superset with Chest Lift (see pg 26).

5-WAY CRUNCHES

ADVANCED

ONE

- Lie on your back with your legs extended together straight up into the air.
- Clasp your hands behind your neck.
- Slowly curl your upper body toward your knees, exhaling softly as you curl. Remember not to pull your neck up with your arms.
- Hold for a count of 1 second, then inhaling, lower yourself until your shoulder blades touch the floor. This completes 1 repetition.
- Perform 10-15 repetitions.

TWO

- Without pausing, spread your feet apart in the air and perform 10-15 more repetitions.

THREE

- Without pausing, bend your knees 90 degrees (your legs are still apart) and perform 10-15 more repetitions.

FOUR

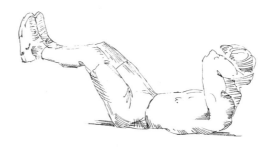

- Without pausing, bring your knees together and perform 10-15 more repetitions.

FIVE

- Without pausing, lower your feet to the floor with your knees still bent and perform 10-15 final repetitions.

HARD ROCKS

Once you are capable of performing the advanced level abdominal exercises, add the Hard Rocks to your routine and **perform in addition to** the 5-Way Crunches and the Intermediate-Advanced Oblique Curl.

❑ **Lie on your back and place your hands palms down under your hips. Your head should be lifted off of the floor (Use a large pillow for support if your neck fatigues easily).**

❑ **Extend your legs straight up in the air.**

❑ **Exhaling softly, squeeze your abdominal muscles and push your hips and legs 4-6 inches higher in the air.**

❑ **Hold for 1 second then return to the start position as you inhale.**

❑ **Repeat until fatigue.**

THE POINTER

Projections show that 92% of Americans are destined to suffer from chronic back pain. Soreness in the lower back also ranks as the most common complaint among riders. Your lower back muscles work continuously during riding to stabilize your upper body and absorb the natural concussions created by your horse in motion. The facts reveal that the majority of "bad backs" are caused by poor posture, weak lower back muscles, and weak abdominal muscles. Fortunately, relief for these back problems can be attained through sensible exercise. The Pointer will strengthen your back muscles and hip flexors, improve your balance, and enhance your muscle awareness. This will eventually enable you to maintain a proper riding position longer without experiencing lower back strain and soreness. It may also keep you from becoming another "bad-back" statistic.

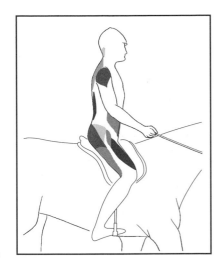

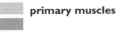

primary muscles

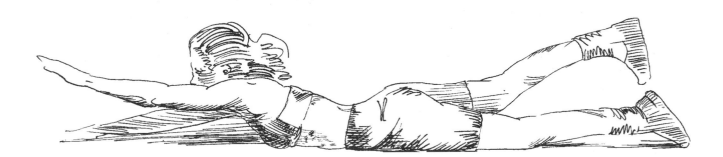

❏ **Lie on your front with your arms and legs extended.**

❏ **Slowly raise your left arm and right leg as high as is comfortable. It should take a count of 10 seconds to raise your arm and leg.**

❏ **Breathe normally and hold this position for a minimum of 15 seconds.**

❏ **Slowly lower your arm and leg (for a count of 10) to the floor.**

❏ **Repeat steps 1 and 2 with your opposite arm**

and leg. This completes 1 repetition.

❏ **Perform a minimum of 3-5 repetitions per set.**

❏ **Perform 2 sets.**

SUPERSET
30 min. workout: Superset with Crunches (see pg 20).
45 min. workout: Superset with Crunches (see pg 20).
60 min. workout: Superset with Crunches (see pg 20).

CHEST LIFT

INTERMEDIATE

- ❑ **Lie on your front with your legs extended.**
- ❑ **Clasp your hands behind your neck.**
- ❑ **Lift your face off the floor and hold.**
- ❑ **Slowly raise your chest until it is barely above the floor.**
- ❑ **Keep your toes on the floor during the lift.**
- ❑ **Return to start and repeat for a minimum of 10 repetitions.**
- ❑ **Perform 2 sets.**

SUPERSET

30 min workout: Superset with **The Seated Fly** (see pg 38).

45 min workout: Superset with **The Seated Fly** (see pg 38).

60 min workout: Superset with **Crunches** (see pg 21).

THE ADVANCED POINTER   ADVANCED

- ❏ Lower yourself onto all fours, placing your hands and your knees shoulder-width apart.

- ❏ Face the floor and hold your back in a flat position (neither swayed nor arched) by tightening your abdominal and lower back muscles. This places your back in a safe "neutral" position and increases the efficiency of the exercise.

- ❏ Slowly raise your left arm and right leg for a count of 10 seconds until both are fully extended and parallel to the floor. Breathe normally and maintain this position for a minimum of 15 seconds.

- ❏ Slowly lower (for a count of 10) your arm and leg to the floor.

- ❏ Repeat with your opposite arm and leg. This completes 1 repetition.

- ❏ Perform a minimum of 3-5 repetitions per set. To increase difficulty, you can perform additional repetitions, wear ankle weights, riding boots, or ski boots, etc.

- ❏ Perform 2 sets.

SUPERSET
30 min. workout: Superset with The Seated Fly (see pg 38).
45 min. workout: Superset with The Seated Fly (see pg 38).
60 min. workout: Superset with Crunches (see pg 22).

ADDUCTOR LIFT

In the forward seat, your adductors are used in cueing and collecting your horse, forming the primary basis for support. In balanced set, your adductors are used independently to cue and to stabilize your upper and lower body. Regardless of your riding style and degree of fitness you will need to strengthen your adductors in order to physically improve as a rider. The Adductor Lift is designed to build strength and muscular endurance in your inner thighs.

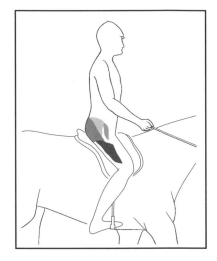

primary muscles

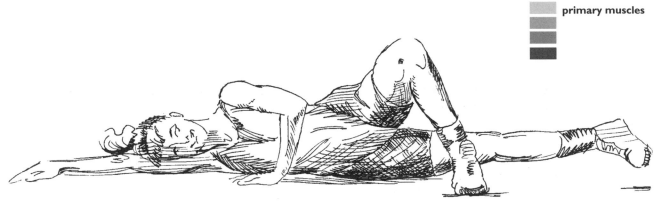

- ❑ Lie on your right side with your legs straight and your head supported by your extended right arm.
- ❑ Place your left hand flat on the floor in front of your chest for balance.
- ❑ Cross your upper leg over your extended lower leg and place your foot flat on the floor.
- ❑ Slowly raise your lower (right) leg a comfortable distance off the floor - this may be only a few inches. Breath normally and hold for a count of 3 seconds. Keep your body straight, do not bend at the hips.
- ❑ Finish the lift by slowly lowering your leg in a smooth and controlled manner.

- ❑ Repeat until you reach fatigue.
- ❑ Switch sides and perform exercise with your left leg for an equal number of repetitions. This completes 1 set.
- ❑ To increase difficulty, perform additional repetitions, wear ankle weights, riding boots, or ski boots, etc.
- ❑ Perform 2 sets.

SUPERSET

30, 45, and 60 min. workouts: Superset with **The Squeeze** (see pg 30).

ADDUCTOR FLYS

ALTERNATE

- ❏ Lay on your back with both legs pointed up toward the sky. Your hands should be placed palms down beneath the small of your back.

- ❏ Open your legs as wide as they will comfortably go, then bring them inward 6 inches.

- ❏ Now gently pulse back and forth within this range for 5 seconds.

- ❏ Return to the start position. This is 1 repetition.

- ❏ Repeat until fatigue.

- ❏ Perform 2 sets.

- ❏ To increase the difficulty of this exercise, pulse for longer than 5 seconds, perform more repetitions, wear ankle weights or heavy boots.

THE SQUEEZE

UNIVERSAL

The Squeeze also builds strength and muscular endurance in your adductor muscles. Why have 2 exercises for the same muscle group? Because our riding instructors are always instructing us to drop our stirrups and ride in a 2-point position for what seems an eternity. Instructors are never satisfied . . . and with good reason. Few riders are gifted with sufficient strength and muscular endurance in their adductors.

To perform The Squeeze you will need a basketball, volleyball, or soccerball.* The secret to this exercise is to underinflate the ball slightly so it gives a little. This will increase your comfort and efficiency.

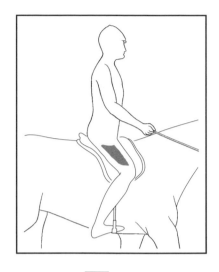

primary muscles

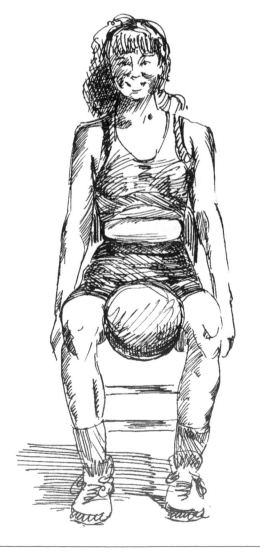

- ❏ **Sit in a chair with your feet shoulder width apart.**
- ❏ **Place a ball (basketball, volleyball, soccerball, etc.) between your legs just above the knees.**
- ❏ **Squeeze and hold for 7 seconds.**
- ❏ **Relax for 3 seconds.**
- ❏ **Repeat for a minimum of 10 repetitions or until fatique.**
- ❏ **Perform 2 sets.**

* You can also perform this exercise standing with your knees bent, squeezing a large pillow, or sitting in a saddle on a saddle rack.

SUPERSET

30, 45, and 60 min. workout:s Superset with Adductor Lift (see pg 28).

HAMSTRING LIFT

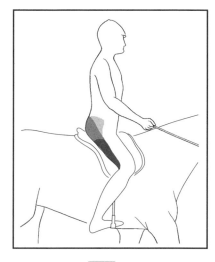

Your hamstrings flex your legs at the knees enabling you to walk, run, and sit. Hamstrings play more of a secondary role in riding. They help you mount and dismount your horse, maintain correct leg position in the saddle, and post the trot. The Hamstring Lift will improve your strength and muscular endurance and maintain critical muscle balance in your legs (combined with the Quad Lift) .

What is "muscle balance" and why is it a big deal? Antagonistic muscles such as your hamstrings and quadriceps need to be equivalent in strength for you to maintain healthy joints. For example, if your hamstring is stronger than your quadricep (or vice-versa), then your knee is pulled out of its natural alignment making it more vulnerable to injury and chronic problems.

primary muscles

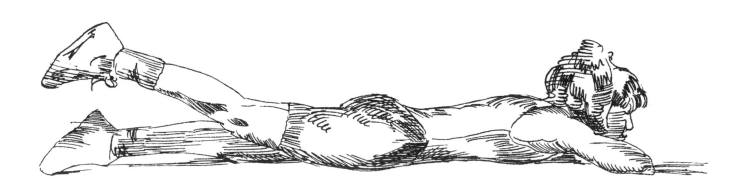

- ❑ **Lie on your front with your legs extended and your chin resting on your hands.**
- ❑ **Raise your right leg 1 foot off the floor.**
- ❑ **Hold for 1-3 seconds. Breathe normally throughout the entire exercise.**
- ❑ **Relax. It is important to keep your hips firmly on the floor as you perform this exercise.**
- ❑ **Repeat until fatigue.**
- ❑ **Repeat exercise with your left leg for an**

equal number of repetitions. This completes 1 set.
- ❑ **To increase the difficulty of this exercise, perform additional repetitions, wear ankle weights, riding boots, or ski boots, etc.**
- ❑ **Perform a total of 2 sets.**

SUPERSET
45, and 60 min. workout: Superset with Quad Lift (see pg 32).

QUAD LIFT

Your quadriceps enable you to extend your legs at the knees, making them the antagonistic muscles to your hamstrings . . . as one muscle contracts the other relaxes and lengthens. Like the hamstrings, your quadriceps allow you to walk and run, to mount and dismount, to keep your legs in a correct fore-hind riding position, and to post the trot. The quad lift will build strength and muscular endurance in your quadriceps. You'll have to excuse the nagging . . . , but remember to always exercise your quadriceps and hamstrings equally so that one doesn't become stronger than the other.

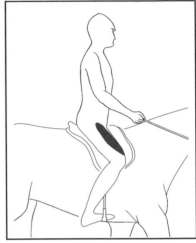

■ **primary muscles**

❏ **Sit on the floor with your legs extended in front of you. Support yourself with your hands slightly behind you on the floor.**

❏ **Breathe normally and slowly raise your right leg 8-14 inches above the floor with your toes pointing skyward. Focus on squeezing your quadricep muscle as you lift.**

❏ **Hold for 1-3 seconds then lower.**

❏ **Repeat with your left leg for an equal number of repetitions. This completes 1 set.**

❏ **To increase the difficulty of this exercise, perform additional repetitions, wear ankle weights, riding boots, or ski boots, etc.**

❏ **Perform 2 sets.**

SUPERSET

45, and 60 min. workout: Superset with Hamstring Lift (see pg 31).

HALF KNEE SQUATS

ALTERNATE

☐ Stand with your feet shoulder width apart and your knees bent slightly. Check for good posture throughout your back.

☐ Bend your knees and lower yourself as far as you can without lifting your heels off the floor (Don't go lower than a 90 degree bend in your knees . . . any lower will stress your knees).

☐ Hold for 1 second. Look straight ahead and focus on your hamstrings as you exercise. Do not fully straighten your legs when you return to the start position.

☐ Repeat for a minimum of 20 repetitions or until fatigue.

☐ Perform 2 sets.

HEEL RAISE

UNIVERSAL

The Heel Raise will build strength and muscular endurance in your gastrocnemius and soleus muscles. Although calf-flexibility is more important to you as a rider-athlete, strength training is necessary to maintain adequate muscle balance in your legs. You will need to improvise a suitable step for this exercise. A set of stairs, a raised doorway, or any stable object that is at least 5 inches off of the ground will suffice. You will also need a nearby wall or post to balance against.

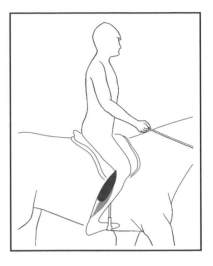

■ **primary muscles**
□

❑ **Stand with the balls of your feet and your toes on the step, and balance yourself with your hands.**

❑ **Raise up on your toes as far as you can go.**

❑ **Breathe normally and hold for 1 second.**

❑ **Gently drop your heels as low as they will comfortably go.**

❑ **Hold for 1 second then raise your heels again. Focus on and squeeze your calf muscles as you raise and lower. Be sure that your movements are smooth and controlled.**

❑ **This completes 1 repetition.**

❑ **Repeat until fatigue.**

❑ **Perform 2 sets.**

SUPERSET

60 min workout: Superset with Oblique Curl (see pg 35).

OBLIQUE CURL

BEGINNER

Your obliqes enable you to rotate at the waist and to pull (flex) yourself up when you are behind vertical in a sitting position. This is critical to your ability as a rider to maintain balance in the saddle. Your obliques also (along with your other abdominal muscles) help stabilize your pelvis which enables you to maintain good posture. An additional benefit is that tight obliques contribute to the appearance of a trim waist.

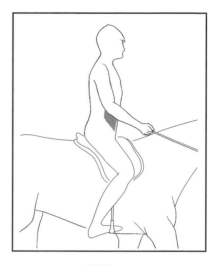

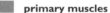 primary muscles

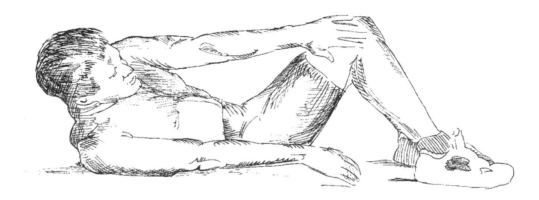

- ❑ Lie on your back with your knees bent and your feet flat on the floor. Place your hands at your sides or between your legs. Hold your head as if you're clutching a racquetball under your chin.
- ❑ Exhaling softly, slowly curl up (twisting slightly counter-clockwise and squeezing those oblique muscles) and extend your right hand past your left knee until your shoulder blades are off the floor.
- ❑ Lower yourself (inhaling softly) until your shoulder blades touch the floor.
- ❑ This completes 1 repetition.

- ❑ Repeat until you reach fatigue.
- ❑ Repeat exercise with your left hand extending past your right knee.
- ❑ This completes 1 set.
- ❑ Perform 2 sets.

SUPERSET
30 min. workout: Superset with Crunches (see pg 20).
45 min. workout: Superset with Crunches (see pg 20).
60 min. workout: Superset with Heel Raise (see pg 34).

OBLIQUE CURL

INTERMEDIATE

- ❑ Lie on your back and bend your knees.
- ❑ Fold your arms across your chest.
- ❑ Touch your right elbow to your left knee or until your shoulder blades are off the floor.
- ❑ Hold for a count of 1 second then lower yourself until your shoulder blades touch the floor.
- ❑ Repeat until fatigue.

- ❑ Repeat with your left elbow to your right knee to complete 1 set.
- ❑ Perform 2 sets.

SUPERSET
30 min. workout: Superset with **Crunches** (see pg 21).
45 min. workout: Superset with **Crunches** (see pg 21).
60 min. workout: Superset with **Heel Raise** (see pg 34).

OBLIQUE CURL

ADVANCED

- ❏ Lie on your back and bend your knees.
- ❏ Clasp your hands behind your neck.
- ❏ Curl and twist toward your left knee until your shoulder blades are off the floor. Do not pull your neck up with your arms.
- ❏ Hold for a count of 1 second then lower yourself until your shoulder blades touch the floor.
- ❏ Repeat until fatigue.

- ❏ Repeat exercise with your left elbow to your right knee to complete 1 set.
- ❏ Perform 2 sets.

SUPERSET
30 min. workout: **Superset with Crunches** (see pg 22).
45 min. workout: **Superset with Crunches** (see pg 22).
60 min. workout: **Superset with Heel Raise** (see pg 34).

THE SEATED FLY

UNIVERSAL

Poor posture is a major problem among riders as well as the general public. Individuals in both cases subconsciously collapse their chests and round their shoulders. Bad posture in the saddle can cause poor balance, fatigue, and improper cueing. The major contributors to poor posture are laziness and weak back muscles which allow your chest and shoulders to roll forward. The Seated Inverted Fly addresses this problem by developing strength and muscular endurance in your trapezius and posterior deltoid muscles, and by laterally stretching your chest muscles. This will help you improve your posture and attain a taller riding position through increased upper body control and muscle awareness. You will also improve your overall balance by "pulling" your upper body into correct alignment with your lower body.

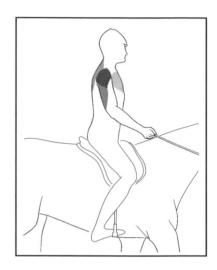

primary muscles

secondary muscles

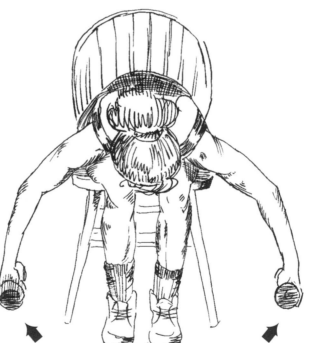

- ❏ You will need 2 small dumbbells (or other alternative weights such as soup cans, etc.) for this exercise. Your "dumbbells" should be a comfortable weight that is easy for you to lift.

- ❏ Sit in a chair or on a bench with your knees bent and your feet spaced comfortably apart on the floor.

- ❏ Place your chest on your thighs and gently lower your arms out to the side.

- ❏ Slightly bend your elbows and face the floor (this will place your head in a neutral position and minimize any unnecessary stress on your neck).

THE SEATED FLY (cont.)

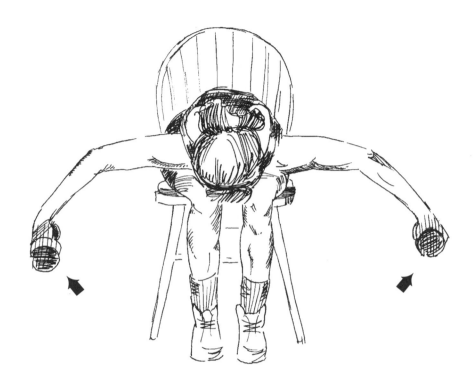

- Keeping your elbows bent, gently raise both arms as high as you can. Focus on the muscles between your shoulder blades and try to squeeze and feel them contract as you raise your arms. Visualizing your muscles at work as you exercise can greatly increase the quality of your exercise.

- Hold this position for 3 seconds then slowly lower your arms back to the relaxed position. Breathe normally throughout this exercise and keep your chest on your thighs at all times.

- Repeat for a minimum of 10 repetitions or until fatigue.

- Perform 2 sets.

SUPERSET

30 min. & 45 min. workout: Superset with The Pointer, Chest Lift, or The Advanced Pointer (see pgs 25-27).

60 min. workout: Superset with Wall Pushes, Kneeling Push-ups, or Push-ups (see pgs 40-42).

WALL PUSHES

Wall Pushes provide another ingredient in your posture building formula. Improving the strength in your pectoralis major will maintain adequate muscle balance with your upper back muscles. Secondary emphasis is placed on your triceps.

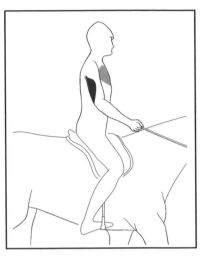

primary muscles

- ❏ Position yourself one and a half arm's length from a wall.
- ❏ Stand with your feet together, lean forward and place both hands chest high and shoulder width apart on the wall. Your elbows should be slightly bent.
- ❏ Bend your elbows and lean as far as you can into the wall. Breathe normally.

- ❏ Slowly push yourself away from the wall and back to the start position. Focus on and squeeze your chest muscles.
- ❏ Repeat for a minimum of 15 repetitions or until fatigue.

SUPERSET

60 min. workout: Superset with The Seated Fly (see pg 38).

KNEELING PUSH-UPS INTERMEDIATE

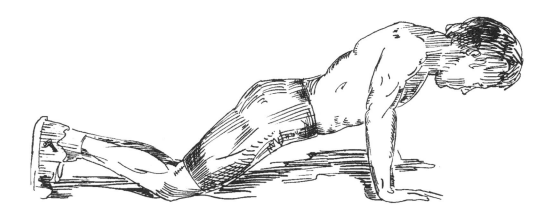

- ❑ Lower yourself onto your hands and knees with your hands shoulder-width apart.
- ❑ Bending at the elbows and inhaling softly, lower your upper body until your nose almost touches the floor.
- ❑ Keep your back straight.
- ❑ Hold for 1 second.

- ❑ Exhaling slowly, push yourself until your arms are almost fully extended.
- ❑ Repeat until fatigue.
- ❑ Perform 2 sets.

SUPERSET

60 min. workout: Superset with **The Seated Fly** (see pg 38).

PUSH-UPS

ADVANCED

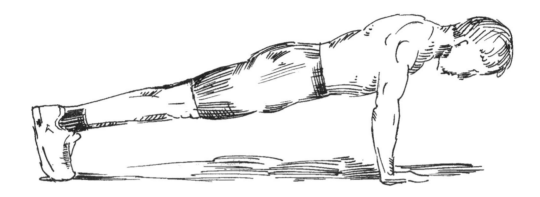

- ❑ Lie on your front with your legs extended and your hands shoulder-width apart on the floor.
- ❑ Exhaling slowly, push up onto your hands and toes until your arms are almost fully extended.
- ❑ Keep your back and legs straight.
- ❑ Hold for 1 second.
- ❑ Inhale softly, bend at the elbows and lower to an inch above the floor.

- ❑ Hold for 1 second then push up again.
- ❑ Repeat until fatigue.
- ❑ Perform 2 sets.

SUPERSET

60 min. workout: Superset with **The Seated Fly** (see pg 38).

FORWARD ARM RAISE

UNIVERSAL

The Forward Arm Raise builds muscular endurance in your anterior deltoid which will benefit your posture and will help you avoid using your reins and your horse's mouth for support. But you never lean on your horse's mouth . . . Are you sure, oh-leaden-arm-one? Many riders subconciously rely on a little extra counter-tension in their reins to support their arms and shoulders.

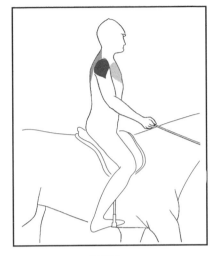

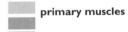
primary muscles

❑ **You will need 2 small dumbbells for this exercise. They should be light enough for you to lift easily for the first few repetitions.**

❑ **Stand with your feet shoulder width apart and your knees slightly bent.**

❑ **Start with your hands down at your sides and your palms facing each other.**

❑ **Breathing normally, slowly raise your right arm until it is parallel to the floor. As you raise your arm, turn your hand counter-clockwise (supinate) until your palm faces the floor.**

❑ **Hold for 1 second. Slowly lower your arm down to your side (start position).**

❑ **Now raise and supinate your left arm. Lower.**

❑ **This completes 1 repetition.**

❑ **Repeat until fatigue.**

❑ **Perform 2 sets.**

SUPERSET

60 min. workout: Superset with Wrist Swing (see pg 44).

WRIST SWING

The Wrist Swing is the first of the Good Hands exercises. It is designed to help you develop softer and more precise hands in the saddle by building strength and muscular endurance in the brachioradialis muscles in your fore-arms, by reinforcing correct hand-wrist-arm positioning (enabling you to avoid rolling your hands over), and by improving your muscle awareness.

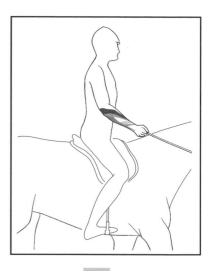

primary muscles

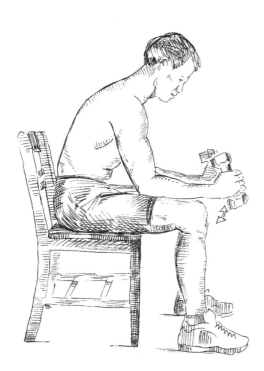

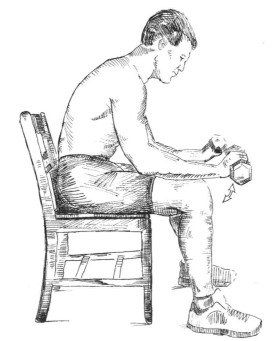

❑ **You will need light-weight dumbbells and a bench for this exercise.**

❑ **Sit on the bench and rest your forearms on your thighs.**

❑ **Holding the dumbbells with your palms facing each other, slowly swing your wrists up and down until you reach fatigue.**

❑ **Rotate your palms until facing the floor.**

❑ **Slowly swing your weights up and down until you again reach fatigue. (Repeating the exercise with your palms down works your wrist extensors for muscle balance.) Your movements should be smooth and con-trolled.**

❑ **This completes 1 set.**

❑ **Perform a total of 2 sets.**

SUPERSET

60 min. workout: Superset with Forward Arm Raise (see pg 43).

KICK-BACKS

UNIVERSAL

Your triceps' function is to extend your arms at your elbows. The Kick-backs will improve the strength and muscular endurance in your triceps and will help you maintain correct muscle balance with your biceps.

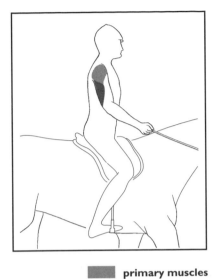

■ primary muscles

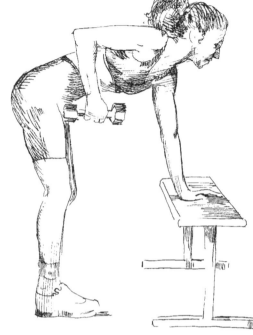

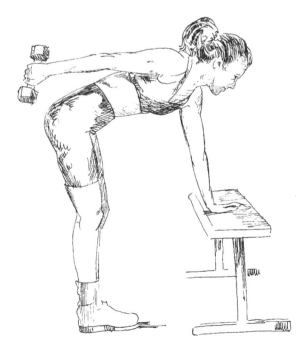

❑ **Bend over and lean against a chair or bench with your left hand. Your back should be parallel to the floor and your knees bent. Grasp the dumbbell in your right hand and bend your elbow until your right upper arm is parallel to the floor and your elbow is tucked close to your side. This is your start position.**

❑ **Keeping your upper arm motionless, slowly straighten your arm to full extension. Focus on and squeeze your tricep especially at the top of your motion.**

❑ **Hold for 1 second, then return to the start position.**

❑ **Repeat until fatigue.**

❑ **Repeat with your left arm for an equal number of repetitions to complete 1 set.**

❑ **Perform 2 sets.**

SUPERSET

60 min. workout: Superset with Rotation Curl (see pg 47).

OVERHEAD EXTENSIONS ALTERNATE

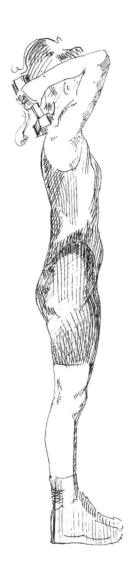

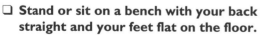

- ❑ Stand or sit on a bench with your back straight and your feet flat on the floor.
- ❑ Holding the dumbbell in your right hand, raise your right arm straight above your head.
- ❑ Support your right arm with your left hand by grasping your right upper arm just below the elbow.

- ❑ Slowly bend your right arm at the elbow until your forearm is parallel to the floor.
- ❑ Return to full extension.
- ❑ This completes 1 repetition.
- ❑ Breathe normally and squeeze your tricep throughout each repetition.
- ❑ Repeat until fatigue.
- ❑ Repeat with your left arm for an equal number of repetitions to complete 1 set.
- ❑ Perform 2 sets.

ROTATION CURL

Your biceps and your brachialis flex your arms at your elbows and assist in shoulder flexion (raising your arm) and in shoulder adduction (moving your arm across your body). The Bicep Rotation Curl adds strength and muscular endurance from 2 separate angles, working both your biceps and your brachialis muscles.

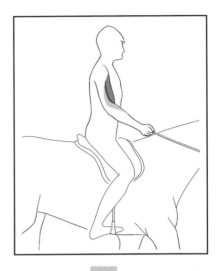

 primary muscles

- ❏ **Stand with your feet shoulder width-apart and your knees slightly bent.**
- ❏ **Hold a dumbbell in each hand and let your arms hang at your sides with your palms facing each other.**
- ❏ **Flexing at the elbow, raise the right dumbbell toward your shoulder.**
- ❏ **Keep your elbow as stationary as possible and exhale as you curl.**
- ❏ **Rotate your palm up toward the sky as you near the halfway point of your curl.**
- ❏ **Squeeze your bicep throughout the entire curl.**
- ❏ **When you reach the top, squeeze for 1 second then slowly lower your dumbbell.**
- ❏ **Repeat with your left arm to complete 1 repetition.**
- ❏ **Repeat until fatigue.**
- ❏ **Perform 2 sets.**

SUPERSET

60 min. workout: Superset with Kick-backs (see pg 45).

HAMMER CURL

ALTERNATE

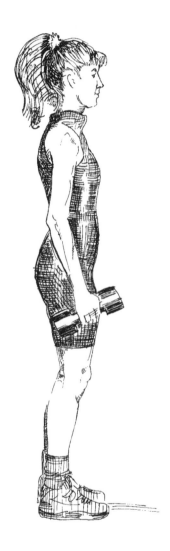
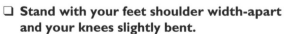
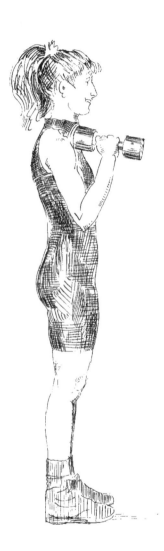

❏ Stand with your feet shoulder width-apart and your knees slightly bent.

❏ Hold a dumbbell in each hand and let your arms hang at your sides. As in the Rotation Curl, your palms should face each other.

❏ Flexing at the elbow, raise the right dumbbell toward your shoulder.

❏ Keep your elbow as stationary as possible and exhale as you curl.

❏ Keep your thumb toward the sky and your palm facing inside as you curl.

❏ Squeeze your bicep throughout the entire curl.

❏ When you reach the top squeeze for 1 second then slowly lower your dumbbell.

❏ Repeat with your left arm to complete 1 repetition.

❏ Repeat until fatigue. Perform 2 sets.

ORANGE CRUSH

UNIVERSAL

Heavy hands combined with a negative attitude in the saddle only serves to injure and toughen your horse's mouth. However, adequate strength in your hands and forearms can enhance the development and effective use of soft-precise hands in the saddle. The Orange Crush will add strength and muscular endurance to your forearms, and improve the strength, muscular awareness, and dexterity in your hands. Combine good hands with a positive and patient mental approach and eventually you and your horse will have fewer differences-of-opinion.

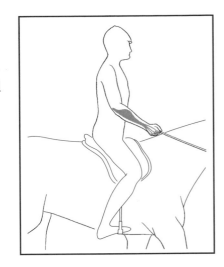

▓ **primary muscles**

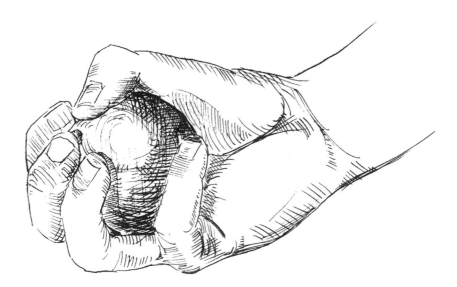

❏ **Grasp a tennis ball in your right hand.**

❏ **Squeeze and hold for 1 second, then release.**

❏ **Repeat until fatigue.**

❏ **Perform an equal number of repetitions with your left hand to complete 1 set.**

❏ **Perform a total of 2 sets.**

SUPERSET

60 min. workout: Superset with Steeple (see pg 50).

STEEPLE

UNIVERSAL

The problem with holding a pair of reins is that the movement in your fingers must be very subtle or control of the reins shifts from your hands-wrists to your shoulders-upper arms. The result: You overreact in your cues. The Steeple is derived from a traditional children's game. It works to develop dexterity and muscular awareness in your fingers. This will improve the precision in your hand movements helping you become more accurate in your cues and more responsive to your horse's mouth.

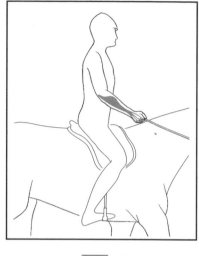

primary muscles

❑ **Hold your hands together and align the corresponding fingers.**

❑ **Separate your palms with your fingers still touching.**

❑ **Lift your thumbs apart and hold for 1 second, then touch them together again.**

❑ **Lift your index fingers apart and hold for 1 second, then return . . . lift your middle (3rd) fingers apart, hold, return . . .**

lift your ring (4th) fingers apart . . .
lift your little (5th) fingers apart . . .

❑ **Repeat for 1 minute.**

❑ **This completes 1 set.**

SUPERSET

60 min. workout: Superset with Orange Crush (see pg 49).

REIN WALK

You will need a pair of reins for this exercise.

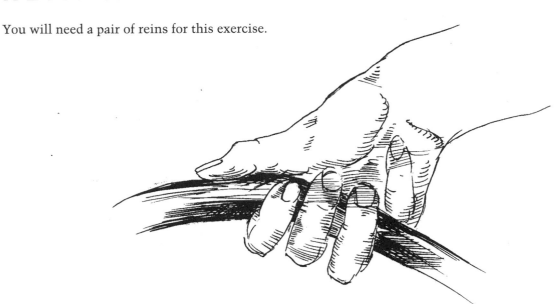

❑ **Grasp the reins gently with both hands, placing your thumbs and little fingers on the top of the reins and your other fingers on the bottom side.**

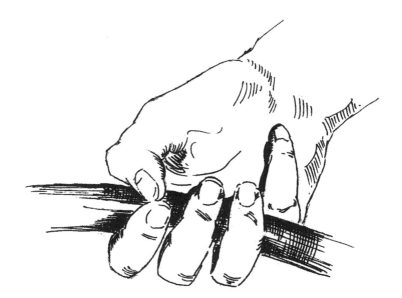

❑ **Now bend your thumbs and slide your fingers and slowly "walk" the reins through your fingers.**

❑ **Continue exercise for at least 1 minute.**

❑ **Perform a total of 2 sets.**

SEAT-SPECIFIC EXERCISES

Several of the riding styles targeted in this book present physical challenges unique to that particular seat. To meet these demands, *The Equestrian Workout* offers three seat-specific exercises on pages 53-55 designed to help you enhance the physical qualities unique to your specific style of riding.

Targeted riding styles include:

- Forward seat (hunter, jumper, english pleasure, etc.)

- Balanced seat (dressage, western, gymkhana, etc.).

- Saddleseat.

Choose the one exercise that applies to your style of riding. This will conclude your strength and muscular endurance exercises. Follow immediately with the flexibility-posture and balance exercises.

Forward Seat

EXTREME SKIER

UNIVERSAL

Forward seat riders commonly sway their backs when riding over fences and during posting. Unfortunately, holding this position quickly fatigues the muscles in your lower back which is a primary reason why the most common complaint among forward seat riders is lower back soreness. The Extreme Skier further addresses this problem by providing additional exercise to build critical muscle endurance in your lower back and hips. Secondary emphasis is in your quadricep muscles.

(Note: Strong abdominal muscles share the load of holding your back and pelvis in correct position, so work hard on your abdominal exercises.)

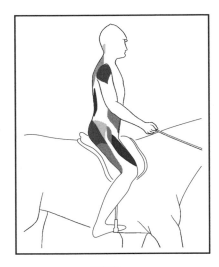

 primary muscles

- ❏ **Stand with your feet shoulder-width apart and your knees bent to a 45 degree angle.**
- ❏ **Position your hands in front of your body as if you were holding a pair or reins.**
- ❏ **Push your butt out behind you and sway your back. Breathe normally and focus on the muscles in your lower back.**
- ❏ **Hold this position for a minimum of 1 minute.**

Balanced Seat

ABDUCTOR LIFT

UNIVERSAL

As a balanced seat rider, you are occasionally faced with opening your upper legs while maintaining sufficient lower leg contact to encourage your horse to relax and move forward at the same time. This can be a physically difficult cue to perform. While you do not need to be a contortionist to pull this off, you do require sufficient flexibility throughout your body and adequate strength in your outer thigh muscles (abductors). The Abductor Lift works to build strength and muscular endurance in your abductors.

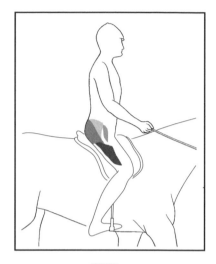

 primary muscles

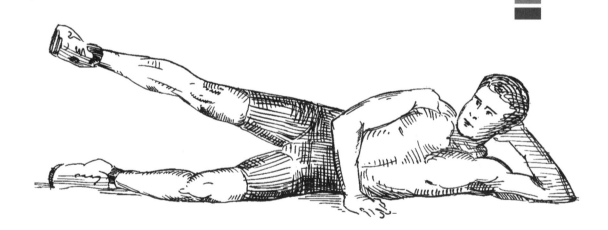

- ❑ **Lie down on your left side with your right (upper) leg fully extended.**
- ❑ **Your left (lower) leg should be bent at the knee and your hips should be in a vertical line.**
- ❑ **Slowly lift your right (upper) leg as high as is comfortable.**
- ❑ **Hold for 1 second then lower to complete 1 repetition.**

- ❑ **Breathe normally and squeeze your abductor muscle as you exercise.**
- ❑ **Repeat until you reach fatigue.**
- ❑ **Roll over and repeat exercise with your left leg for an equal number of repetitions.**
- ❑ **Perform 2 sets.**

Saddleseat

FLARED LEG LIFT

UNIVERSAL

Saddleseat riders must ride with a unique leg position opposite to other styles of riding: The inside edges of your feet are flared out. This requires considerable flexibility along the inside of your ankle and increased strength along the outside of your ankle. The Adductor Stretch and Ham Stretch are also particularly beneficial for saddleseat riders.

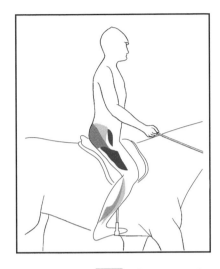

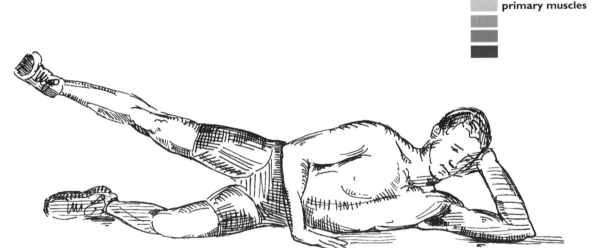

■ **primary muscles**

- ❏ **Lie down on your left side with your legs extended. Your hips should be in a vertical line.**
- ❏ **Lift your right (upper) leg a comfortable distance off of the floor.**
- ❏ **Point the inside edge of your foot and your heel as you lift your leg.**
- ❏ **Hold for 1 second, then lower.**
- ❏ **Repeat until fatigue.**
- ❏ **Repeat exercise with your left leg for an equal number of repetitions.**

(Note: Here is an excellent exercise you can perform in addition to the Flared Leg Lift:

You will need a bicycle tube or surgical tubing tied in a loop. Sit in a chair and place your foot in the tubing. Pull to increase the tension. Start with your foot turned in then slowly turn your foot out as far as is comfortable. Repeat until you reach fatigue then perform the exercise with your other foot.)

Type 2:
Flexibility, Posture & Balance

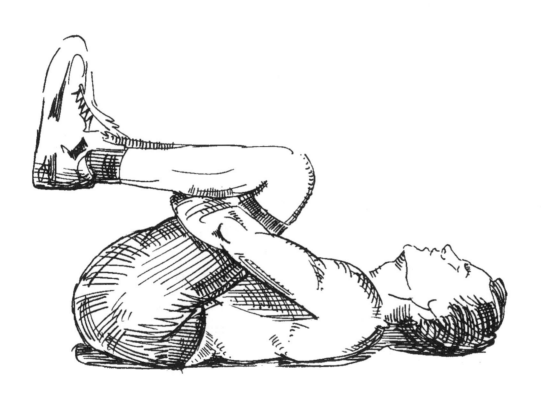

INTRODUCTION

Flexibility & Posture

Improved flexibility is the cornerstone of your success as a rider-athlete:

- It reduces the potential for injuries. Increased flexibility enables your body joints to with-stand greater impact-shock when your body encounters an unyielding surface . . . such as the ground.

- It contributes to improved athletic perfor-mance. The rider-athlete with good flexibility has greater freedom of movement in all direc-tions, and can more easily change the direction of a movement, decreasing the chance of a fall, and the chance of injury when a fall occurs.

The Equestrian Workout emphasizes a highly effective and safe form of "static stretching." This is stretching your muscle to the point of mild discomfort and holding that position for at least 45 seconds.

- The minimum stretching time of 45 seconds is emphasized because when you attempt to stretch, sensory impulses from your central nervous system cause your muscle to contract and resist the stretch for 30 seconds. Only after you have held the stretch continuously for 30 seconds are new sensory messages released causing that muscle to finally relax and lengthen.

Here are some guidelines to successful stretching:

- Gently hold your stretch. Never bounce.

- Begin with an easy stretch, then proceed to moderate stretches.

- Avoid severe stretching. You should experience only mild discomfort during stretching, never sharp pain.

- Breathe in a relaxed and rhythmic manner. Never hold your breath.

- *Stretch Every Day.* Studies show that only daily stretching will produce any significant improvement in flexibility.

Balance

You will conclude with the balance exercises on pages 76 - 85. The first and foremost comment on balance is simply: You can never have enough!

Helpful balancing hints:

- Successful balancing requires mental focus and correct breathing techniques which allow you to relax. Breathing techniques are detailed on page 111.

- Always look straight ahead, never down at your feet.

- Keep your knees bent slightly.

- If you are having trouble balancing, don't get frustrated. Slow down, relax, breathe deeply, and keep trying. Eventually you will succeed!

DORSAL FLEX

The average American and by extension the average rider is woefully weak and inflexible in his/her lower back muscles. So, it's not surprising that the most common complaint among competitive equestrians is chronic pain in the lower back. Maintaining correct riding posture strains your lower back muscles to the point of fatigue, and every stride of your horse transmits tiny shock waves through your lower back and up your spine. So how do you avoid chronic lower back pain? The answer is: Increase your abdominal and back strength, muscular endurance, and flexibility.

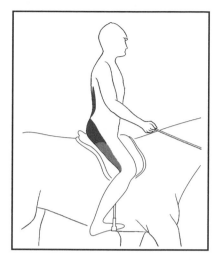

The Dorsal Flex is designed to stretch your lower back muscles and hip flexors with a secondary emphasis in your hamstrings and quadriceps. Increased flexibility will reduce fatigue and soreness in your lower back and will help you develop a deeper riding seat.

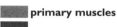 **primary muscles**

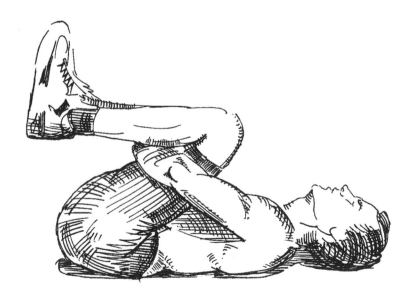

- ❏ Lie flat on your back with your legs extended. Your breathing should be relaxed and rhythmic.
- ❏ Slowly bring both knees to your chest, clasping the back of your thighs with your hands.

- ❏ Focus on the stretch in your lower back muscles as you gently pull your knees further into your chest.
- ❏ Hold this position for a minimum of 45 seconds.

CROSSLEGGED BOW INTERMEDIATE-ADVANCED

❑ Sit crosslegged on the floor.

❑ Sit as tall as you can up on your seat bones . . . this will help you maintain correct posture.

❑ With your hands on your knees, slowly bend forward at the hips . . . keep your back straight as you flex gently forward.

❑ Hold for a minimum of 45 seconds.

❑ After stretching in position 1 for 45 seconds, lower your head, relax, and let your back round up toward the sky.

❑ Extend your arms forward and gently reach toward the floor.

❑ Hold this position for another 30 seconds.

VENTRAL STRETCH

BEGINNER

The previous exercise, The Fold Flex, stretches your back dorsally. The Ventral Stretch is designed to stretch your lower back in a "ventral" or frontal direction. Why stretch both ways? Because your back needs to be equally flexible in both directions to allow you to move freely through a full range of motion and to comfortably maintain correct posture.

Here's a fact to remember: Most back problems are at least partially caused by dorsal/ventral inflexibility. Consequently, this workout focuses heavily on properly stretching and conditioning your back so that you may spend quality time in the saddle for many years to come.

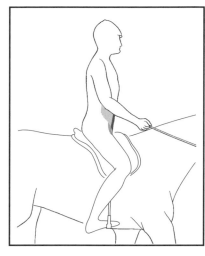

primary muscles

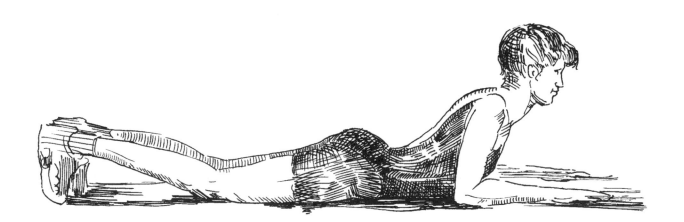

❑ Lie face down on the floor.

❑ Place your hands shoulder width apart and parallel with your face.

❑ Keeping your hips firmly on the floor, gently sway your back and raise up onto your elbows and forearms.

❑ Breathe in a slow and rhythmic manner to help yourself relax and remember to concentrate on your back muscles as you stretch.

❑ Hold this position for at least 45 seconds.

VENTRAL STRETCH INTERMEDIATE-ADVANCED

❑ Assume the same position shown in the beginner Ventral Stretch. **Shift your weight off of your elbows and onto your hands and slowly raise your elbows off of the floor for a deeper stretch.**

❑ **The more you straighten your arms, the more of a stretch you will experience.**

❑ **Remember to keep your hips on the floor, focus, and breathe in a relaxed, rhythmic manner.**

ANGRY CAT & SWAY-BACK HORSE

UNIVERSAL

Poor posture is an common equestrian condition. Riders often collapse their chests and round their shoulders forward instead of sitting "tall" in the saddle. Contributing causes to poor posture are a lack of muscle awareness, inflexibility across the chest, weak back muscles, and inflexibility though the entire back. All of these areas will be addressed in this workout, but we'll concentrate on back inflexibility for one more exercise. One of the best methods for increasing your overall back flexibility is a traditional children's exercise called the Angry Cat & Sway-back Horse. This exercise will stretch muscles dorsally the entire length of your back, and ventrally through your abdomen. As you perform this exercise you'll quickly understand how it earned its name.

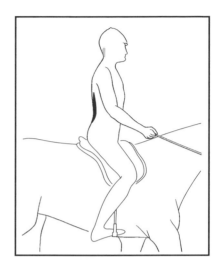

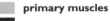 **primary muscles**

❑ **Lower yourself onto all fours, placing your hands and your knees shoulder width apart.**

❑ **Slowly arch your back toward the sky until you have reached as far as you can go. Face the floor to minimize stress on your neck. This is the "Angry Cat" position. (Note: Spitting and clawing are not required for authenticity's sake, although they may prove to be effective stress relievers and/or self-defense mechanisms.)**

❑ **Hold this position for a minimum of 45 seconds, then proceed directly to step 2.**

❑ **Starting from the Angry-Cat position, gently sway your back down towards the floor until you have comfortably reached the limit of your range of motion.**

❑ **Face slightly forward to minimize stress on your neck. This is the "Sway-back Horse".**

❑ **Breathe normally and hold this position for a minimum of 45 seconds.**

HIP STRETCH

Your hip extensors allow you to extend your legs at your hips, enabling you to perform necessary functions such as walking and mounting your horse. The Hip Stretch is designed to stretch your hip extensors with secondary emphasis in your gluteus medius. Improved flexibility in your hip extensors will help you develop a deeper seat for riding.

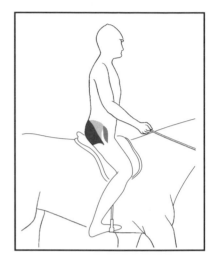

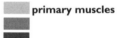

primary muscles

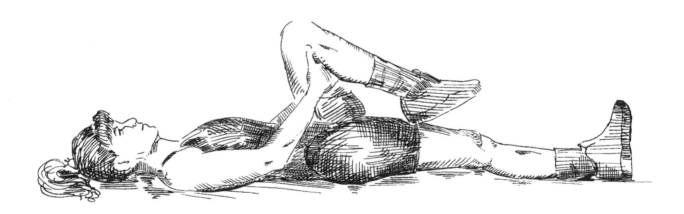

- ❏ Lie flat on your back with your legs extended.
- ❏ Keep your head flat on the floor.
- ❏ Clasp the back of your left thigh with both hands and slowly bring your knee towards your chest as far as it will comfortably travel.
- ❏ Hold for a minimum of 45 seconds.
- ❏ Breathe normally and try to visualize your hip flexors and lower back muscles relaxing and lengthening as you gently hold your stretch. Remember, never rock back and forth during a stretch, all stretching should be slow and controlled.
- ❏ Gently return your left leg to the extended position.
- ❏ Repeat the stretch with your right leg.

STARTER'S STRETCH

Your hip flexors are the antagonistic muscles to your hip extensors and perform the opposite action. As the name implies, your hip flexors enable you to flex your leg at the hip, which allows you to walk, run, and lift your leg into a stirrup. The Starter's Stretch stretches your hip flexors with secondary emphasis in your quadriceps. As with your hip extensors, improved flexibility in your hip flexors will help you develop a deeper seat for riding.

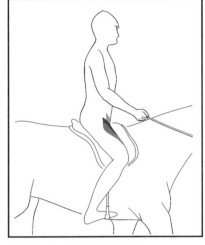

 **primary muscles**

INTERMEDIATE/ ADVANCED

- ❏ **Kneel down on your left knee with your right foot flat on the floor in front of you.**
- ❏ **Slowly lean forward and place your hands on either side of your right foot.**
- ❏ **Your right knee will raise slightly off the floor at this point.**
- ❏ **Hold this position for at least 45 seconds.**
- ❏ **Repeat with your left foot forward.**

- ❏ **Assume the Starter Stretch position detailed above, but place both hands on the inside of your forward foot. This will enable you to lower your upper body a few more inches for a deeper hip flexor stretch.**

SEATED HAM STRETCH

UNIVERSAL

Your hamstring acts as a large bicep between your knee and hip and enables you to flex your leg at the knee. It plays a crucial role in daily activities such as walking and running. While it is not one of the primary muscles used during riding, it is employed whenever you attempt to lengthen your leg and lower your heel in the stirrup. In addition, it is necessary to stretch and strengthen your hamstrings to maintain adequate leg muscle balance and overall fitness.

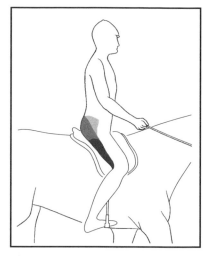

primary muscles

- ❑ Sit down on the floor with both legs stretched in front of you.
- ❑ Slide your right foot up your left leg until it rests next to your left knee. Keeping your back straight and bending only at the hips, slowly reach for your left ankle with both hands. Try to feel your left hamstring relaxing and lengthening as you stretch. Remember, stretch only until you feel mild discomfort (never pain!) in your hamstring, and don't bounce!
- ❑ Hold this position for a minimum of 45 seconds.
- ❑ Relax and repeat with your right hamstring.

STANDING HAM STRETCH ALTERNATE

- ❑ For this exercise you will need to use an object that is knee to hip high such as a chair, table, or even 2 stacked hay bales.

- ❑ Place your left foot on top of the object, keeping your left leg as straight as you can. It is **OK** to bend slightly at the knees if you must.

- ❑ Slowly bend forward at the hip (keep your back straight), look straight ahead, and reach for your ankles with both hands. All motion should be smooth and controlled.

- ❑ Hold for a minimum of 45 seconds, then stretch your right hamstring.

QUAD STRETCH

UNIVERSAL

Your quadricep is the antagonistic muscle to your hamstring, performing the opposite action of extending your leg at the knee. You use your quadricep during riding whenever you post a trot or "lengthen" your leg in the saddle.

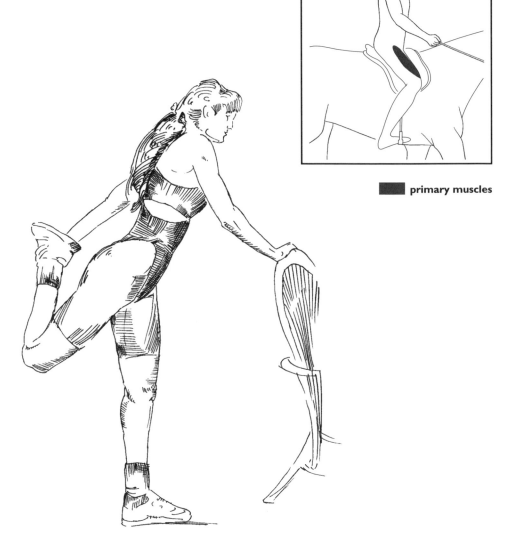

primary muscles

- ❑ Stand next to a wall or post and use your right hand to maintain your balance.
- ❑ Bend your right knee and grasp your right ankle with your left hand.

- ❑ Slowly pull your heel up and away from your buttocks until you feel a stretch in your quadricep muscle.
- ❑ Hold this position for a minimum of 45 seconds.
- ❑ Lower and repeat with your left leg.

SUMO STRETCH

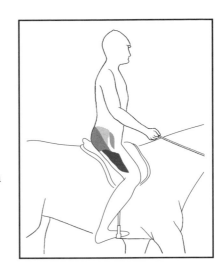

Your "adductors" or inner thigh muscles help you maintain your balance when standing, walking, or running, a role that goes largely unnoticed and doesn't require a great deal of endurance or strength. Consequently, most individuals' adductors are weak and under-developed. During riding, your adductors play a starring role requiring a great amount of endurance and strength. Flexibility is needed to reduce the amount of stress and fatigue your adductors incur when applying some of that strength during leg-cueing, collection, riding in a forward seat, or when you're just hanging on for the ride.

(Note: For those of you with visions of traditional wrestling fame, this is an opportune moment to stamp your feet and growl something menacing in Japanese.)

primary muscles

❑ **Stand with your feet spread wide apart and place your hands above your knees.**

❑ **Keeping both soles of your feet planted firmly on the floor, gently shift your weight onto your right leg, bend your right knee and straighten your left knee. (Do not bend your left knee past 90 degrees as this will** place additional and unnecessary stress on your knee joint.)

❑ **Breathe normally and attempt to feel your adductor muscle as it lengthens.**

❑ **Hold steadily for a minimum of 45 seconds, then repeat with your right leg extended.**

ADDUCTOR STRETCH

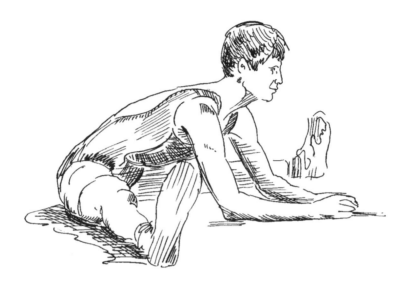

- ❑ Sit on the floor and spread your legs apart.
- ❑ Your knees should be straight.
- ❑ Slowly bend forward at the hips, keeping your back straight and your head up.
- ❑ Breathe in a relaxed and rhythmic manner and focus on your adductor muscles as they begin to lengthen. As with many other body parts, your adductor muscles can become strained rather easily so be smart and stretch gently and patiently.
- ❑ Hold this position for a minimum of 45 seconds.

PUSH-THE-WALL-DOWN

UNIVERSAL

Anyone who has taken riding lessons knows well the incessant bark of the instructor commanding them to lower their heels. The inability to maintain a proper heel angle is a result of inflexible calf muscles. Push-the-Wall-Down will improve your flexibility in your gastrocnemius muscles which are the most recognizable part of your calves.

The combination of this exercise and the Soleus Stretch (next page) will enable you to develop a greater range of motion and help you maintain a correct riding form which may satisfy even your riding instructor.

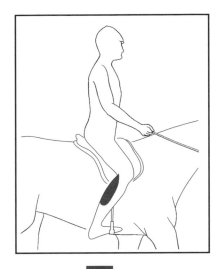

primary muscles

- ❏ **Place your hands shoulder-width apart against a wall with your elbows bent slightly.**
- ❏ **Bend your right knee and fully extend your left leg as far as you can behind you with your left heel firmly on the floor. Both feet should be pointed straight ahead.**
- ❏ **To stretch, slowly lean towards the wall. Remember to keep your heels flat on the floor at all times.**
- ❏ **Hold this position for a minimum of 45 seconds.**
- ❏ **Repeat with your right leg behind your left.**

SOLEUS STRETCH

The Soleus Stretch is designed to increase your flexibility in your other calf muscle, the lesser known but highly important soleus.

Successful track and field athletes have learned that the most effective method of improving calf flexibility is to separately stretch the gastrocnemius and soleus muscles. Equestrians athletes can benefit greatly from this knowledge as well.

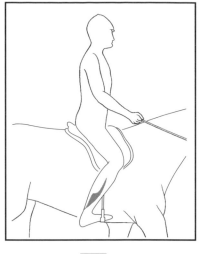

primary muscles

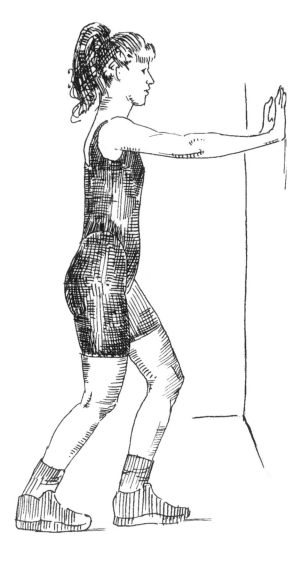

❑ **Place your hands shoulder-width apart against a wall. Your elbows should be slightly bent.**

❑ **Position your right foot comfortably behind your left foot with your right heel firmly on the floor. Both feet should be pointed straight ahead.**

❑ **Bend slowly at your knees, stopping as soon as your right heel begins to lift off of the floor. Do not permit your heel to actually rise, it is important to keep it flat on the floor to gain full benefit of this exercise. All of your movements should be smooth and controlled.**

❑ **Breathe normally and hold this position for a minimum of 45 seconds.**

❑ **Repeat with your left leg behind your right.**

CORNER FLEX

The Corner Stretch is designed to improve your posture by increasing the flexibility in your pectorals (chest) and anterior deltoids (front shoulder). When combined with strengthening exercises for your upper back this exercise will help you break the habit of rolling your shoulders forward and collapsing your chest when you ride.

(Note: definition of the trainer's seat: legs overbent, body slanted forward, elbows pointed out, shoulders rounded, chest collapsed, and eyes down. Quote this to your trainer at your own peril!)

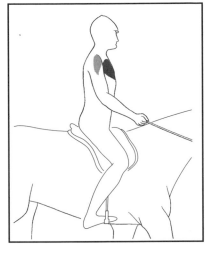

 primary muscles

❑ **Stand facing the inside corner of a wall.**

❑ **Place your hands on each side of the wall shoulder width apart and shoulder height.**

❑ **Gently lean into the corner. You should feel compression between your shoulder blades and slight stretching across your chest.**

❑ **Hold this position for a minimum of 45 seconds.**

7TH INNING STRETCH

ALTERNATE

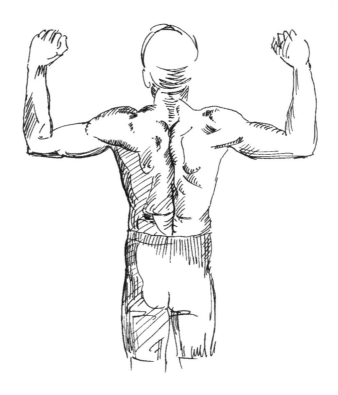

- ❏ Maintaining good posture, stand or sit on a chair or the floor.
- ❏ Raise your arms out to your sides.
- ❏ Bend your elbows 90 degrees with your fingers pointing up and your upper arms parallel to the floor.

- ❏ Simultaneously bring both arms back and squeeze your shoulder blades together. You should also feel a slight stretch across your chest.
- ❏ Hold this position for at least 45 seconds.

REACH-FOR-THE-SKY

UNIVERSAL

At first glance this posture exercise appears to be extremely easy. But it may surprise you, it's tougher than it looks. Reach-for-the-Sky is designed to increase the flexibility primarily in your upper back with secondary emphasis in your chest. So, you're wondering how flexibility affects your posture? Stretching effectively extends your range of motion which enables you to maintain good posture more comfortably. As a result, you will maintain better posture more consistently. (Similar to a domino effect.) Reach-for-the-Sky also serves as an excellent test to occasionally gauge your posture level.

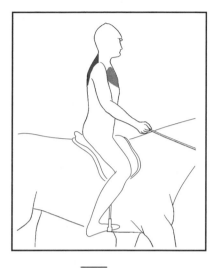

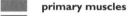 **primary muscles**

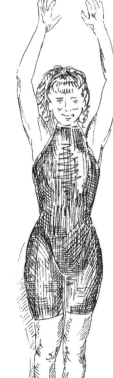

❑ **Stand with your back against a flat wall with your elbows pointing out to the sides and your hands pointing up. Now here begins the tough part.**

❑ **Touch the wall on 5 points:**
the heels of your feet
your buttocks
your shoulders
your elbows
the top of your hands

❑ **If you can't touch on all 5 points, get as close as you can and proceed with the exercise. Attempt to keep your back straight throughout the entire exercise.**

❑ **Slowly slide your hands up as high as you can reach and lightly touch your index fingers together.**

❑ **Breathe normally and hold this position for a minimum of 45 seconds.**

(Note: Any resemblence to the position assumed by victims of the medieval torture device known as "the rack" is purely coincidental.)

THE STORK

A highly developed sense of balance is among the most important qualities possessed by the average person and the successful rider. Without it you would be unable to sit, stand, or walk, much less ride a horse. The ability to balance is created from a combination of muscle awareness, muscle conditioning, and electrical signals to/from your central nervous system. Effective balance is not a given trait, it is learned and developed. Inactivity breeds poor balance. On the other hand, focused training produces excellent balancing ability.

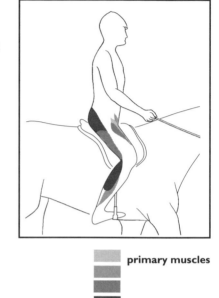

primary muscles

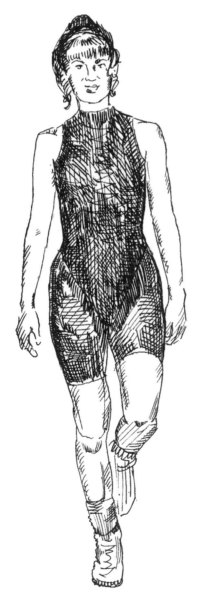

Prepare for balancing by performing the Really Old Relaxation Technique on page 79.

❑ **Stand with your feet shoulder-width apart and your knees unlocked.**

❑ **Face forward and let your arms hang at your sides.**

❑ **Shift your weight to your left leg and slowly raise your right foot off of the floor. It's hard, but try to avoid the temptation to look down at your feet, and do not allow your legs to touch each other.***

❑ **Breathe normally and attempt to balance for a minimum of 1 minute.**

❑ **Repeat, raising your left foot.**

THE STORK

Prepare for balancing by performing the Really-Old Relaxation Technique on page 79.

- ❏ **Assume the same position detailed for the beginner Stork on the previous page.**
- ❏ **Shift your weight onto your left leg and raise your right foot off the floor.**
- ❏ **Turn your palms outward and inhale gently as you slowly raise both arms out from your sides until you bring your palms together high above your head.**

THE STORK

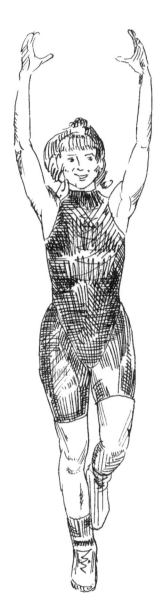

For an advanced level balancing exercise, perform the beginner Stork (on page 76) with your eyes closed. Sound easy? You may be surprised.

❑ **Rotate your palms out.**

❑ **Exhaling softly, gently lower your arms back to your sides.**

❑ **Repeat 6 times without lowering your raised foot to the floor.**

❑ **Repeat the entire exercise with your left foot raised.**

* The Ten-Toe Conspiracy:

When your legs touch they communicate, conspire, and assist each other in responding to the demands encountered during an activity such as balancing. (Similar to cheating during your biology exam.) This makes a balancing exercise easier, but less efficient in improving your skills.

REALLY-OLD RELAXATION TECHNIQUE

This simple but effective breathing exercise has its roots in ancient arts such as Yoga, Tai Chi, and Aikido. You will use it as part of this workout to prepare yourself for balancing. Proper breath control enhances your ability to balance by helping your body and mind relax. This will enable you to focus (and balance) more effectively:

❏ **Stand with your feet shoulder-width apart and your knees unlocked. Let your arms hang at your sides and focus your eyes forward.**

❏ **Slowly inhale as deeply as you can. Allow your shoulders to gently rise with each intake of breath.**

❏ **Exhale slowly and let your shoulders drop softly as a feather. Imagine your physical and mental stress being carried out on each expulsion of breath. Feel the tension drain from your body and from your mind.**

❏ **Repeat at least 3 times.**

Note: Use this relaxation technique anytime you feel tense.

STANDING BALANCE BOARD

ALTERNATE - BEGINNER

The Standing Balance Board offers a challenging alternative to The Stork. As the name implies, it requires an easily-constructed prop called a balance board. For instructions on how to construct a balance board, see ***Building A Balance Board*** on p. 119.

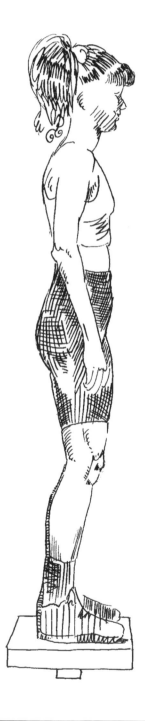

Prepare for balancing by performing the Really-Old Relaxation Technique on page 79.

- ❏ **Place the balance board on the floor with the beam running left-right.**

- ❏ **Center your feet on the board. Your feet should be approximately shoulder-width apart, and your knees should be unlocked.**

- ❏ **Let your arms hang lazily at your sides.**

- ❏ **Focus your eyes straight ahead. (Pretend you are standing on the high-dive at the swimming pool for the first time: Don't look down!)**

- ❏ **Breathe normally, and remember . . . by relaxing your body and your mind you will enhance your ability to balance.**

- ❏ **Attempt to balance for for a minimum of 1 minute.**

- ❏ **Repeat the exercise with the balance board running front-back.**

Feeling frustrated with your attempts to balance? Simply take 2–3 long, deep breaths, exhale slowly, R-E-L-A-X, and try again. Eventually you *will* succeed.

STANDING BALANCE BOARD ALTERNATE - INTERMEDIATE

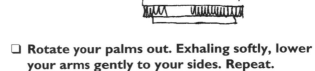

❑ Center yourself on the board as detailed in the beginner Standing Balance Board on the previous page.

❑ Turn your palms outward and inhale gently as you raise both arms slowly from your sides until your palms touch high above your head.

❑ Rotate your palms out. Exhaling softly, lower your arms gently to your sides. Repeat.

❑ Attempt to balance for a minimum of 1 minute while performing steps 1 & 2.

STANDING BALANCE BOARD

ALTERNATE - ADVANCED

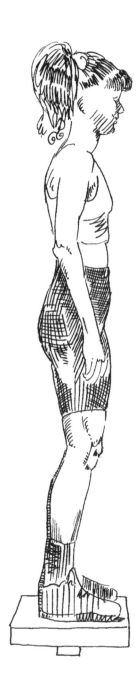

For an advanced level balancing exercise,
perform the beginner Standing Balance Board
with your eyes closed.

KNEELING BALANCE BOARD   BEGINNER

The Kneeling Balance Board offers a sport-specific balancing exercise by lowering your center of gravity and encouraging you to utilize your upper legs and seat for balance. This exercise requires the use of a balance board (see *Building A Balance Board*, p. 119) and a small, soft pillow.

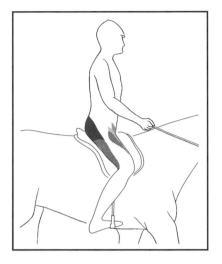

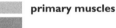 **primary muscles**

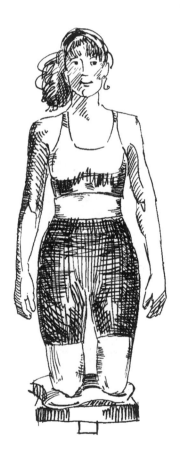

- ❏ **Using the pillow as a cushion, kneel on the balance board with the center beam running front to back between your knees.**

- ❏ **Space your knees shoulder width apart.**

- ❏ **With your arms at your sides, raise your feet off of the floor and attempt to balance on your knees for a minimum of 1 minute.**

- ❏ **Focus your eyes straight ahead and breathe normally.**

- ❏ **As you become more adept at balancing, attempt to balance longer—up to 3 minutes.**

Discontinue immediately if you experience any knee pain or have a history of knee problems.

KNEELING BALANCE BOARD INTERMEDIATE

❑ Center yourself on the board as detailed in the beginner Kneeling Balance Board on the previous page.

❑ Turn your palms outward and inhale gently as you raise both arms slowly until your palms touch high above your head.

❑ Rotate your palms out.

❑ Exhaling softly, gently lower your arms until your fingertips touch the floor.

❑ Repeat.

❑ Attempt to balance for a minimum of 1 minute while performing steps 1 & 2.

KNEELING BALANCE BOARD   ADVANCED

For an advanced level balancing exercise,
perform the beginner Kneeling Balance Board
with your eyes closed.

Aerobic Exercise

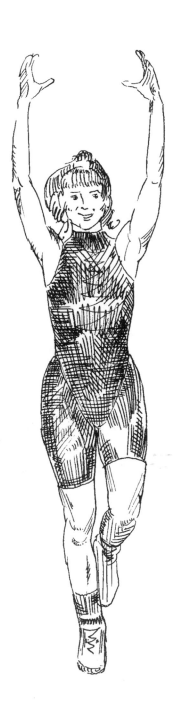

AEROBIC EXERCISE

Feeling a bit tired after your ride? Perhaps a little winded after climbing a flight of stairs? These are signs that you need to improve your endurance through aerobic exercise. Aerobic training affects your cardiorespiratory endurance by elevating your heart rate over an extended period of time. Here's how it works:

During sustained exercise your muscles depend upon oxygen to properly metabolize carbohydrates and fats into energy. Your heart pumps oxygenated blood to your muscles delivering the needed oxygen. When your heart is unable to keep up with your muscles' demand for oxygen you begin to experience fatigue. Consistent aerobic exercise turns your heart into a more efficient pumping mechanism by enabling it to pump more oxygenated blood with each stroke.

Consequently, aerobic training can combat fatigue and improve your energy level by increasing the rate at which your body can transport and utilize oxygen during exercise.

The key to aerobic exercise is to participate in a variety of activities. Varying your fitness routine will help you keep exercise fun and effective for the rest of your life. Choosing from aerobic activities such as walking, jogging, cycling, low-moderate impact aerobics classes, step bench, stair climbing, swimming, rowing, skating, and cross-country skiing can help keep you fit year-round in any climate. Another benefit from varying your exercises is that you receive a cross-training affect. This tunes your muscles to different movements and different intensities, resulting in less likelihood of injury, especially repetitive motion injuries, and in greater overall athleticism.

Here are some considerations concerning aerobic exercise:

- To improve your cardiorespiratory endurance you should participate in an aerobic exercise at least 3 times a week and no more than 6 times a week. You can participate in aerobic activities on the same days you perform your strength-flexibility-balance workout or on alternate days.

- Each aerobic workout should last for at least 20 minutes of continuous activity with your heart rate raised to your target level.

Monitoring Your Heart Rate

The intensity of your effort during exercise is a critical factor in improving your endurance and overall fitness. Your pace can be too fast or too slow. To receive the maximum aerobic benefit for

> **When you rest, your heart pumps an average of 5 liters of blood per minute. When you exercise, your muscles consume oxyen at a much faster rate, forcing your heart to pump faster and to pump more oxygenated blood per heartbeat . . . up to an estimated 20 liters of blood per minute (or up to a whopping 30 liters per minute for an elite endurance athlete).**

your effort you should monitor your heartbeats-per-minute periodically during exercise and maintain your heart rate within 70% - 85% of your maximum heart rate. This heart rate zone is known as your exercise target zone.

The most effective and reliable means of monitoring your exercise heart rate is with an electronic heart rate monitor that attaches to your chest with an elastic belt. However, if you don't have access to a heart rate monitor, you can manually count your heartbeats and refer to the chart on p. 90. Here are some key terms that will help you track your heart rate:

Aerobic target zone - This is the heart rate zone that is most effective for receiving cardiorespiratory benefits.

Exercise heart rate - Your "target" heart rate that is optimum for the benefits of aerobic exercise.

Fat-burning zone - This is the heart rate zone that is most effective for "burning fat".

Maximum heart rate - The maximum number of times your heart can contract in one minute.

Resting heart rate - The number of heartbeats per minute when you are at complete rest.

Safety heart rate - The heart rate suggested for beginner exercisers is 60% of their maximum heart rate. This is the minimum amount of stress you can place on your heart and still benefit from aerobic exercise.

Taking your heart rate:

As you exercise, periodically count your heartbeats for 15 seconds and multiply by 4. Refer to the chart to see if your heart rate is in your target zone. The trick to this is to not stop exercising while you monitor your heart rate. (If you stop, your heart rate immediately begins to fall and you will not get an accurate reading) If it falls below your target level, then you need to intensify your exercise effort. If it is above your target zone, then you are exercising too hard and you need to slow down.

Training Effect:

With consistent exercise your heart becomes a more efficient pump during periods of increased exertion. It pumps more blood with each stroke while your heart rate is reduced.

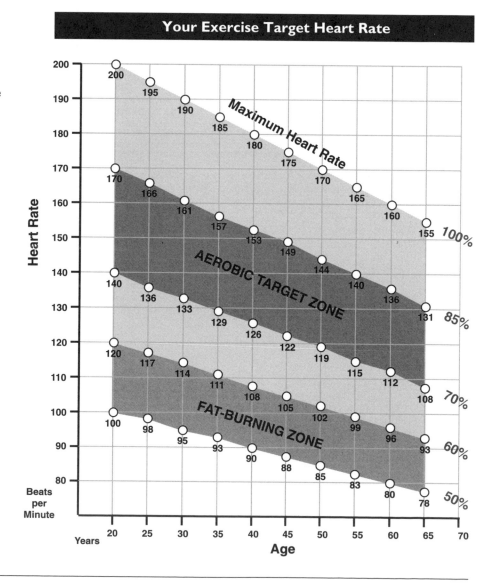

Your Exercise Target Heart Rate

NUTRITION STRATEGY

NUTRITION STRATEGY

What is a balanced and healthy diet? How will you benefit from good nutrition? Can nutrition improve my performance level in exercise and in competitive riding? To answer these and other nutrition questions *The Equestrian Workout* utilized the extensive resources and expertise of nutrition extension specialist Jennifer Anderson, Ph.D., R.D. of Colorado State University.

Eating For A Healthy Life-style

A healthy diet will supply your body with fuel for energy, regulators for your life-processes, and building materials for growth, maintenance, and repair. These life-long nutritional needs are fulfilled with vital nutrients such as water, carbohydrates (including fiber), fats, proteins, vitamins, and minerals. Ideally, your diet should provide sufficient and balanced amounts of these nutrients, create only the amount of energy you need to maintain your appropriate weight and body composition, avoid excessive intakes of fats, salt, and sugar, offer a variety of foods to choose from, and consist of foods that fit your tastes, life-style, family and cultural traditions, and budget.

The bad news is that the typical American diet falls short of these goals, containing too much protein and fat, and not enough carbohydrates, fiber, and water. The good news is that you can easily correct this nutritional imbalance, and reward yourself with improved health and increased energy.

A balanced diet for you as a wise and enduring adult American should consist of:

- **6-8 glasses (8 oz. each) of water per day** (plus extra for fluid replacement during & after exercise due to sweat loss)

- **57% carbohydrates** (found in potatoes, corn, & other vegetables, pasta, rice, dried beans & peas, breads, cereals, and other grain products)

- **10-12% proteins** (found in fish, meats, poultry, dried beans, peas, soy products, dairy products, eggs & nuts)

- **less than 30% fats** (less than 10% saturated fats, 10% polyunsaturated fats, & 10% monounsaturated fats)

These recommendations remain the same regardless of how active you are, except in extreme cases such as marathon runners who require increased amounts of carbohydrates and proteins. One way to insure that your diet meets your needs is to follow the *Dietary Guidelines*, a nutritional road map for Americans aged 2 years and older. The *Dietary Guidelines* offer the best and most current advice from America's nutrition experts.

Eat a variety of foods

Your body requires over 40 essential nutrients to function properly. No single food supplies all of these nutrients, so it is important to eat a variety of foods from the 5 major food groups to attain an adequate nutritional balance. The 5 major food groups and suggested serving amounts are illustrated in *The Food Guide Pyramid*, an easy-to-use diagram based on the *Dietary Guidelines*. *The Food Guide Pyramid* (page 96) will help you determine the correct balance of foods to eat for good health, and the right amount of servings to maintain healthy weight.

The recommended number of servings in the *Pyramid* are for an entire day, and you should eat at least the minimum number of servings from each food group. Start with plenty of whole-grain breads, cereals, rice, and pasta, add at least 5 servings of vegetables and fruits, 2–3 servings from milk, yogurt, cheese and other calcium sources, and 2–3 servings from meat, poultry, fish, dry beans, eggs, and nuts. No serving size is given for fats, oils, and sweet, because the recommendation is to eat them as little as possible. Remember that fats and sugars naturally occur in all of the food groups as well.

Maintain healthy weight

Being overweight is associated with numerous health problems including high blood pressure, heart disease, stroke, diabetes, and certain forms of cancer. It can also limit your skills as a rider/athlete by negatively affecting your balance, flexibility, muscular endurance, and cardiovascular endurance. Being too thin can lead to an increased risk of osteoporosis in women, and may adversely affect your riding ability through reduced energy reserves resulting in decreased muscular endurance, cardiovascular endurance, and strength. The correct and healthy weight for

you is determined not by total pounds, but by how much of your body is fat or "body fat percentage." A relatively easy and accessible method for measuring your body fat is the skin fold test, in which a clinician uses a caliper to measure the thickness of a fold of skin on the back of your arm, below your shoulder blade, or other areas of your body. To receive a skinfold test, contact your local registered dietitian or family physician.

Your body shape is another important gauge of your health level. Excess fat in the abdomen may pose a greater health risk than extra fat in the hips and thighs primarily because abdominal fat, when mobilized, travels directly to your liver where it is converted into a cholesterol carrying lipoprotein which is known to increase your chances of diabetes and coronary heart disease.

If you want to lose weight you must take in fewer calories than you burn. Any excess energy will be stored as body fat. Successful weight loss

DIETARY GUIDELINES

1. Eat a variety of foods.
2. Maintain healthy weight.
3. Choose a diet low in fat, saturated fat, & cholesterol.
4. Choose a diet with plenty of vegetables, fruits, & grain products.
5. Use sugars only in moderation.
6. Use salt & sodium only in moderation.
7. If you drink alcoholic beverages, do so in moderation.

THE FOOD GUIDE PYRAMID

Developed by the USDA Human Nutrition Information Service & the Food Marketing Institute

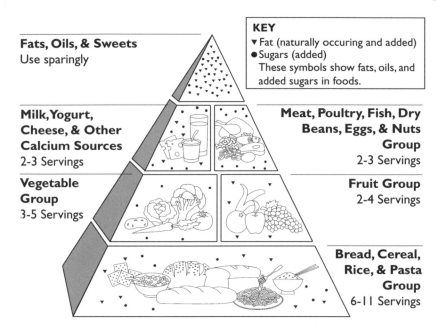

Fats, Oils, & Sweets
Use sparingly

KEY
▼ Fat (naturally occuring and added)
● Sugars (added)
   These symbols show fats, oils, and
   added sugars in foods.

Milk, Yogurt, Cheese, & Other Calcium Sources
2-3 Servings

Meat, Poultry, Fish, Dry Beans, Eggs, & Nuts Group
2-3 Servings

Vegetable Group
3-5 Servings

Fruit Group
2-4 Servings

Bread, Cereal, Rice, & Pasta Group
6-11 Servings

WHAT IS ONE SERVING?
Here are some examples of the amount of food that counts as 1 serving.

BREAD, CEREAL, RICE, AND PASTA	bread	1 slice
	ready-to-eat cereal	1 ounce
	cooked cereal, rice, or pasta	1/2 cup
FRUIT	apple, orange, or banana	1 medium size
	chopped, cooked, or canned fruit	1/2 cup
	fruit juice	3/4 cup
VEGETABLES	raw leafy vegetables (lettuce, spinach)	1 cup
	cooked greens	1 1/2 cups
	other vegetables, cooked or chopped raw	1/2 cup
	vegetable juice	3/4 cup
MEAT, POULTRY, FISH, DRY BEANS, EGGS, AND NUTS	cooked lean meat, poultry, or fish	2-3 ounces
	sardines	6
	cooked dry beans	1 cup
	eggs	2
	peanut butter	4 tablespoons
MILK, YOGURT, AND CHEESE	milk or yogurt	1 cup
	natural cheese	1 1/2 ounces
	process cheese	2 ounces

is accomplished by increasing your physical activity, and by choosing foods with fewer calories, lower fat, and more quality nutrients. In other words, plan your fat loss strategy around the **Dietary Guidelines**, **The Food Guide Pyramid**, and a regular exercise program. You can control overeating by eating slowly, taking smaller portions, and avoiding "seconds." Stay away from crash diets as they are often dangerous, and any positive results are usually only temporary. Effective long-term weight and fat reduction is safely achieved only through good eating and exercise habits.

Choose a diet low in fat, saturated fat, and cholesterol

Fat contains twice the number of calories as an equal amount of carbohydrate or protein, as a result, energy derived from eating fatty foods is much easier to convert to unwanted body fat. Eating foods low in total dietary fat, especially saturated fat, and dietary cholesterol can lower your blood cholesterol to a desirable level and reduce your risk of cardiovascular disease. A blood cholesterol level below 200 mg./dl. is recommended for adults.

Saturated fat is the primary villain in both elevated blood cholesterol and body fat accumulation. Fortunately, saturated fat is easily recognizable: The more saturated a fat is the firmer it is. This rule of thumb applies to animal fats, butterfat, even margarines. Vegetable margarines are more spreadable, but unfortunately more saturated than vegetable oils. This is due to hydrogenation, the hardening process used in the making of margarine. Tropical oils such as palm and coconut oil are also high in saturated fat, even though they don't adhere to the firmness rule. Recommended oils include canola oil, safflower oil, sunflower oil, corn oil, and olive oil. Of course, the best way to eat less saturated fat is simply to eat less total fat.

Dietary cholesterol comes solely from animal-derived foods. While it does affect your blood cholesterol level, it plays a less significant role than total fat and saturated fat. Many cholesterol-containing foods are nutritious, so don't omit them altogether, merely use moderation in your selection and total intake.

Here are a few other suggestions on how to cut down on fats:

- Try baking, broiling, boiling, steaming, and grilling as cooking alternatives to frying, or use nonstick pans with spray-on oil for frying.

- Chicken fat lays primarily under the skin, so remove the skin from the chicken before you cook or eat it. White meat contains less fat than dark meat.

- When shopping for beef or pork, choose lean cuts such as "loin" or "round" from which the fat can be easily trimmed away.

- Drink skim or 2% lowfat milk instead of whole milk. Use no-fat cream cheese or whipped margarine instead of the regular types (whipped contains half the calories).

- Use low-fat yogurt instead of sour cream.

- Use oil-free dressings and reduced calorie mayonnaise.

■ Replace butter or margarine with wine, lemon juice, or broth.

Keep track of your nutritional goals over the entire day instead of for each single meal. It is the amount of fat and calories you have eaten by the end of the day, week, and month that ultimately affects your health.

Choose a diet with plenty of vegetables, fruits, and grain products

You should eat at least 3 servings of vegetables, 2 servings of fruit, and 6 servings of grain products (preferably whole grains) each day. These foods are emphasized for their complex carbohydrates, dietary fiber, low fat content, and other characteristics which contribute to good health. Dietary fiber is found in whole-grain breads and cereals, dry beans and peas, vegetables, and fruits. You should eat a variety of these fiber-rich foods because many differ in the types of natural fiber they contain. A few fiber-rich vegetables, such as lettuce, parsley, and radishes, are so low in calories that they are known as "free foods". Enjoy.

Use sugars only in moderation

Sugars are simple carbohydrates, and supply the same amount of calories as protein (4 cals./gram) and less than half the calories as fat, but sugars are very limited in nutrients. The effects of sugar on a person's weight depends on the individual, however, some people believe that eating small amounts of sugar can trigger enormous eating binges. Sugar also leads to tooth decay, and may cause your energy levels to fluctuate. Enjoy a little.

Use salt and sodium only in moderation

The typical American diet contains excessive salt and sodium. Although sodium is essential to the diet, it is advisable to eat less, especially if you suffer from hypertension, or have a history of high blood pressure in your family. You do not need to make an effort to eat salt and sodium, you get all you need merely by eating a variety of foods.

If you drink alcoholic beverages, do so only in moderation

Alcoholic beverages offer no health benefits, contribute to many health problems, and supply "empty" calories with little or no nutrients.

A word of advice for you and your healthy lifestyle. There isn't anything wrong with indulging yourself occasionally with those treats you enjoy, simply use moderation. Choose your treats judiciously, then eat them for pure pleasure. Meanwhile, choose lowfat, quality foods for your everyday meals.

Nutrition & The Equestrian-Athlete

As an athlete, you will benefit the most from eating complex carbohydrates because your body converts carbohydrates into energy more efficiently than fats or proteins. Carbohydrates are broken down into glucose during digestion, then converted into energy and glycogen. The glycogen is stored in your muscles and liver for future use. During exercise, the stored glycogen is converted back into glucose to provide you with additional energy as you need it.

So, what does this mean for you? It means complex carbohydrates provide you with a convenient source of prolonged, high-octane energy to fuel you through your workout and throughout your day.

- Carbohydrates will provide you with 40-50% of your energy requirement during the early stages of moderate exercise.

- Excess carbohydrates are stored as fat.

- Carbohydrates are found in potatoes, corn, & other vegetables, pasta, rice, dried beans & peas, breads, cereals, and other grains.

- Many high-carbohydrate foods are also great sources of fiber.

Needed fats are converted into energy-providing glycerol and fatty acids. The key phrase here is "needed fats." Unfortunately for modern man and woman, excess fatty acids are easily stored as, you guessed it. . . . body fat . . . , the nemesis of modern man and woman that lurks behind every morsel of food that tastes even remotely edible . . . the taskmaster that forces us to spend endless hours huffing and puffing and sweating into utter exhaustion . . . .

Wait! There is a method to the madness of burning fat. Workouts can be highly effective fat burning tools if you exercise wisely. Using fat as energy depends on the intensity and duration of the exercise, and on your fitness level:

- You will burn more fat during moderate aerobic exercise than during strenuous exercise. Your body uses fat as its primary fuel during low and moderate intensity aerobic exercise. High intensity aerobic exercise causes your body to shift toward anaerobic metabolism and switch from fat energy to carbohydrate energy as your primary fuel. Free fatty acid metabolism will fuel up to 50% of your energy requirement during moderate aerobic exercise such as fast-walking, jogging, or cycling.

- Your bodyfat cells will begin to shrink in size after 20 minutes of moderate exercise, and you will use fat as a primary fuel after 1 hour of prolonged moderate aerobic exercise.

- The fit athlete will use fat for energy more rapidly and more efficiently than the unfit athlete.

Protein is used in building muscle and lean tissue, and to some extent, provides energy. Contrary to popular belief, protein plays only a supportive role in muscle-building. It is the combination of training and your body's use of total calories and quality nutrients that creates muscle. Exercise will not normally increase your need for protein, except in extreme cases such as those of marathon runners.

- Extra protein is stored as bodyfat.

- Excess protein can deprive you of more efficient energy-fuels, and can lead to dehydration as it increases the amount of water required to eliminate your body's waste products.

- A diet of 10-12% protein is sufficient to meet all of your health and fitness needs, and can be met simply by eating a variety of foods.

- Protein is found in fish, meats, poultry, beans, peas, soy products, dairy products, eggs, and nuts.

Eating a varied and balanced diet from the 5 major food groups as illustrated in the **Food Pyramid Guide** will normally assure you of sufficient amounts of vitamins and minerals. There is no medical evidence that eating extra amounts of vitamins will increase your performance level. Minerals, however, play a critical role in fitness and performance, and are affected by prolonged exercise. Strenuous exercise will deplete your body of sodium, potassium, iron, and calcium. These minerals should be replenished by eating normally after exercise or an event.

- Avoid excessive amounts of sodium, including salt tablets and electrolyte drinks. When you sweat, you naturally increase the salt concentration in your body and lower your water content. Excess sodium will absorb additional water from your body cells causing weak muscles, and will lower your potassium level which is needed to regulate muscle activity.

- Women athletes (especially vegetarians) are often prone to iron deficiency, and may find it necessary to supplement iron in their diet. Iron serves to transport oxygen in your blood and your muscles. Iron deficiency anemia impairs oxygen transport which will decrease your aerobic performance and cause you to tire very easily. If you suspect you are iron deficient, contact your physician for testing.

Water is the most critical nutrient for any athlete. Water is present in all of your cells, tissues, and organs. It transports your body's nutrients and waste-products, lubricates your tissues and digestive tract, lubricates and cushions your joints, and regulates your body temperature . . . that is an impressive job description. Any equestrian-athlete can be prone to dehydration, which is the excessive loss of your body fluids. You should start every exercise and event hydrated, and should replace lost body fluids by drinking chilled water or diluted fruit juice at frequent intervals.

- A water loss of just 5% can reduce your performance capacity by 20-30%. Your body loses water primarily through sweating. You may be surprised to know that the next greatest amount of fluid loss is through breathing (water exhaled as vapor).

- The initial symptoms of dehydration are thirst, weakness, then fatigue.

- Chilled fluids are absorbed more rapidly and aid in lowering your body temperature. Sodas, coffee, and tea are not acceptable hydrating fluids. They contain caffeine and sugar, both of which contribute to dehydration. Caffeine acts as a diuretic, causing increased water excretion, and sugar requires additional water to properly absorb into your body's cells.

How do you know you are exercising "moderately"?

An easy rule of thumb is if you cannot talk during exercise, you are working too intensely, so slow down. If you can sing, you are exercising too slowly, so speed up and work harder.

You have the facts, now let's use your nutrition knowledge to maximize your exercise performance level:

- Your pre-workout meal should be high in complex carbohydrates and low in sugar and fat. Eating sugar before exercise or an event will not give you extra energy. It will actually hinder your performance by triggering a surge of insulin which approximately 30 minutes later will cause a sharp drop in your blood sugar level and lead to fatigue.

- Drink plenty of water before, during, and after your workout. Take frequent small sips of water during exercise to keep yourself hydrated. If you wait until you are thirsty, your performance level has already dropped.

- Within 90 minutes after your workout, you need to eat a small carbohydrate-rich snack to replace the carbohydrate fuel you burned during exercise and aid in the recovery process necessary after every workout. A glass of juice and some crackers, or a piece of fruit will suffice.

Now that you've established an exercise routine and diet program for a healthier life-style and improved fitness performance, let's discuss a third area of interest:

Nutritional Strategy for Competitive Equestrian Events

The typical diet of today's rider-competitor at equine events is inadequate to meet the physical and mental demands of competition. The food offered at concessions and fast food restaurants is

Eating a small high carbohydrate meal within 90 minutes after physical exercise will accelerate your body's rate of glycogen storage by 300 percent. This will ensure that you will have sufficient energy for the rest of your activities and for your next workout.

usually high in fat, low in fiber and quality carbohydrates, and contributes only cheap calories incapable of sustaining an adequate energy level throughout the day.

During competition, various factors combine to drain your energy reserves more rapidly than normal, and lower your performance level:

- Competitors endure an elevated emotional stress level throughout the day, with numerous high-stress peaks when involved in several events.

- Repeated physical and mental demands create an additional drain. Riding events require heightened mental awareness and focus, balance, muscular endurance, and occasionally strength and cardiovascular endurance.

- Events are often spread throughout the day, allowing you little time to leave the grounds for a nutritious meal. The amount of time between breakfast and evening meals is longer. Both factors require your energy reserves to last longer than usual.

- Both hot and cold weather can increase the loss of your body fluids.

RECOMMENDED HIGH CARBOHYDRATE "SNACK" FOODS

Some items may have to be prepared ahead.

CARB AMOUNT

32 grams	I apple
27 g	I banana
21 g	I orange
25 g	I pear
61 g	10 pitted dates
57 g	I/2 cup raisins
88 g	I cup dried banana slices
43 g	I cup cranberry-apple juice
38 g	I cup grape juice
24 g	I cup unsweetened grapefruit juice
27 g	I cup orange juice
35 g	I cup peach nectar
61 g	5 dried figs
42 g	4 fig bars
30-33 g	I fat-free snack bar (fruit bar, granola bar, fruit bakes,ect.)
35 g	I bagel (3 I/2" dia.)
33 g	I pita pocket bread (6 I/2" dia.)
13 g	I slice whole wheat bread
45 g	I cup brown rice
35 g	I baked potato with skin
51 g	I baked potato with skin
7 g	I carrot
17 g	I/2 cup corn
39-41 g	I cup kidney or black beans
43-45 g	I cup navy, pinto, or garbanzo beans

As you have probably figured out, your nutritional goal during competition is to maintain a plenty of water.high and consistent energy level throughout the entire day. This will help you remain mentally and physically sharp, and will give you an competitive edge in facing the myriad of obstacles you will encounter. You can control your energy level by formulating a successful nutrition strategy:

1. Begin by drinking plenty of water at least one day in advance. This will help ensure that you are fully hydrated when you begin your show-day.

2. The morning of your show, eat a breakfast that is high in carbohydrates, and low in fat and fiber. The reduced amount of fiber will speed up your digestion, and help you avoid an upset stomach during your events. Again, drink plenty of water.

3. During the day, you should eat small high-carbohydrate "snacks" between your events. As a rule of thumb, you should eat approximately 50 grams of carbohydrates every 2 hours, and drink plenty of water or diluted fruit juice. Diluting the fruit juice will compensate for the juice's sugar content which requires your body to use additional water to absorb the sugar. Prepare or buy your snack foods ahead of time and keep them on hand in a cooler in a convenient location such as your trailer or stall.

THE
MENTAL
ADVANTAGE

THE MENTAL ADVANTAGE

Equine Sports Psychology with Dr. Margot Nacey

The active partnership of human and horse relies extensively upon highly fragile, essential pathways of communication. These pathways carry all of the freely exchanged thoughts, sensations, and emotions manifested in the form of cues and reactions that enable horse and rider to interact and perform. Only through free-flowing two-way communication can the horse-rider partnership learn, develop, and reach a level of understanding necessary for success. Unfortunately, open communication can easily be disrupted and blocked, resulting in a performance breakdown.

The problem is that effective communication can only exist when horse and rider are interacting in a calm and harmonious state. This creates a difficult challenge when your consider that the larger-stronger member of this partnership is acutely tactile and sensitive, therefore easily affected by the slightest change in the rider's mental and physical conditions. Mental disruptions occur in the form of anxiety and, if unchecked, can evolve into the more destructive conditions of fear and anger.

Anxiety can be defined as a state of feeling similar to fear but without an identifiable cause. Anxiety can exist in a generalized state that affects your life on a daily basis over an extended period of time. It can also exist in a situational state and affect the performance of a specific task. When anxiety is situational it is described as "performance anxiety". Its affect on competitive performance depends upon the existing anxiety you bring to the situation and on the stress-causing demands of competition. Performance anxiety can affect you in number of subtle ways or it can quickly push you into an extreme debilitating state through a chain reaction of symptomatic growth.

It is possible to effectively control and overcome your anxieties by improving your mental self-awareness and by developing preventative-therapeutic mental techniques. ***The Mental Advantage*** is a mental practice program developed by Margot Nacey, Ph.D., licensed clinical psychologist, competitive equestrian, and renowned equine sport psychologist. This proven program is designed to help you conquer your performance anxiety, increase your self-awareness, and improve your ability to focus under pressure. Through consistent mental practice you can be on top of your mental game.

Building A Reduced-Stress Foundation

Performance anxiety is specific to a given situation, however it is easily intensified by unrelated stress sources present in other areas of your life. Existing stress and significant changes in your life combine to elevate your overall anxiety level and contribute to your performance anxiety level. Consequently, you must reduce the level of stress in your life outside of competitive sports and create a solid mental-emotional foundation before you can successfully take on your performance anxiety. Any significant event, whether good or bad, can cause additional stress in your life. Stress causing events usually are changes that have taken place within the last year. Examples of significant life-changes include marriage, divorce, death of a friend or loved one, surgery, financial difficulties, change of job, relocation of residence, and difficulties in primary relationships.

The first step is to identify the clues to your significant life-stressors:

- You eat too little or eat too much.

- You sleep too little or sleep too much.

- You're experiencing a loss of energy.

- You're experiencing a lack of interest in things that normally interest you.

- You're experiencing a lack of concentration.

- You dwell on repetitive compulsive thoughts such as:

    "I must not fail at anything. I won't do things unless I can do them well."

    "I should have done that better . . . I can't do anything right."

    "I can't ever please anyone."

    "I wish I could change, but I can't."

    "Everything must be in exactly the right order. Every detail must be perfect."

- You "catastrophize" large and insignificant events into potential disasters.

The influence of change in your life can be overwhelmingly powerful. We tend to discount the power of life-changes because society supports the notion that feelings and emotions are secondary to and are unrelated to our level of functioning. These feelings and emotions must be dealt with before they intensify your anxiety and evolve into negative visualization and into a destructive pattern of self fulfilling prophecy.

While you can not and do not want to avoid certain changes, you can learn to develop a healthy perspective and deal with change productively. Facing the problem is far healthier than denial or running away. When you are stressed and your emotional temperature is running high, the best strategy is to be kind to yourself:

1. Be kind to yourself by recognizing your own limits of time and mental resources. Establish priorities and eliminate the low priority tasks. Use realistic scheduling.

2. Be kind to yourself by reminding yourself of the positives in your life. Negative self talk can turn into a self-fulfilling prophecy.

3. Be kind to yourself by slowing down and allowing yourself to relax. Tackle one task at a time.

4. Don't deny the existence of your problems. Recognize them and take constructive steps to deal with them by looking at your problems objectively, setting goals, and developing a rational step-by-step problem solving strategy.

5. Set realistic expectations. Expectations that are too high can lead to frustration and depression. It's healthy to strive for perfection as long as

you accept the final reality that you can never achieve it.

6. Allow yourself to develop to your full potential as a competitor and as a person by choosing a healthier life-style. Consistent exercise, good nutrition, and a positive mental practice will help you follow a more productive life direction.

7. Promote your rational thoughts such as:

> "There's nothing to worry about."
>
> "I'm going to be o.k."
>
> "Take it one step at a time."
>
> "I know I can complete these tasks."
>
> "I know I can survive this . . .
> I've survived much worse than this."
>
> "I'll give it my best effort and that is good enough."

8. Seek out and discover the logical, productive lesson from each situation. You can learn and benefit from any situation, good or bad.

Identifying Performance Anxiety

The majority of performance anxiety symptoms are initially very subtle and gradually become more apparent as your anxiety builds. Unless you are adept at identifying your initial stress symptoms you can remain unaware of your rising stress level until it reaches an advanced state. When your anxiety grows to this point it is more difficult to control and can have an extreme debilitating effect on your performance.

Learning to recognize the initial clues to your performance anxiety will enable you to identify mounting tension in the early stages and take positive action to alleviate it before it gets out of hand. Initial anxiety symptoms can begin up to 10 days prior to competition. Initial clues to performance anxiety are:

- Sleep disturbances such as a difficulty falling to sleep, waking abruptly, or an inability to fall back to sleep. You may find yourself sleeping too little or too much.

- Bad dreams such as dreams of conflict and nightmares.

- A vague feeling of distress. You experience mood swings, feel anxious and that you are losing control. You're uncomfortable with yourself and hypersensitive to criticism.

- Obsessing on negative events such as the last time you fell off of your horse, blew a lead, forgot your course pattern, etc. Agonizing over past poor performances and projecting future poor performances can create negative self-fulfilling prophecies.

The next step is to develop an awareness of your body's physical tension signals. These are warnings that your body is internalizing mental stress and worry. In most individuals, these physical tension signals will occur repeatedly in the same body location over a period of time. This area of your body is known as your "tension zone" and serves as a reliable and timely clue to building internalized anxiety. For example, a stiff neck or a sore back may be a significant clue that you have internalized your pre-competition performance anxiety. Your body's physical tension signals include:

- Aches and pains.

- Numbness in your hands and feet.

- Somatic symptoms such as headaches, stomach and gastrointestinal pains, and skin, respiratory, and cardiovascular disorders.

Many performance anxiety symptoms may occur during your warm-up or as you enter the ring. Symptoms commonly include muscle tension, sweating, dry mouth, irritability, loss of focus, excessive worry, loss of short term memory, dizziness, difficulty in breathing, and heart palpitations. The scenario may unfold like this:

It is 4–5 hours before your event. You have plenty of time, yet you are feeling irritable and you snap at a friend for an insignificant mistake. You become a little disoriented and your memory is fuzzy. Now, what were you going to do next? . . . and where in the #?#!! did you leave that !#@#! hoof pick? You're feeling dizzy, so you sit down for a moment. You fail to notice that your breathing is becoming more shallow.

It is one hour before your event. You begin warming up your horse. You're worrying that the competition is tough, the arena is a little soggy, and your horse is not performing the way you want. Tension is building in your muscles resulting in a lack of flexibility throughout your body. Of course, your horse immediately senses your inflexibility and your tension build-up and reacts negatively by tensing up himself. You soon notice your horse is not warming up properly and you become more tense, and again your horse senses this and responds with increased tension, which you notice and . . . so on.

It is 15 minutes before your event. You first notice that your stomach is starting to feel real queasy, but soon your lunch is doing things never intended for the human body. You make a mad dash for the nearest bathroom. You're increasingly tense and inflexible, your mouth is now completely dry, and you're sweating as if you were doing the tango in a sauna. Unfortunately, there's more. You've developed a splitting headache, and it's become impossible for you to concentrate (this is no time for a loss of focus). Your breathing is becoming increasingly short and shallow, your heart is beating rapidly (heart palpitations), and the only thing you're visualizing is you and your horse doing the worst "crash-and-burn" this horse show has ever seen!

It is the end of your event and you are leaving the arena. Your ride went poorly. You feel a loss of energy and you are unable to focus on the good parts of your ride. You are thinking only of all the things you and your horse did wrong.

Many equestrians experience some or all of the above stress symptoms, engage in negative visualization, and in an example of self-fulfilling prophecy, set the stage for yet another frustrating performance. However, this does not have to be you. It is possible to climb out of negative self-fulfilling prophecies and towards a healthier life and better performance by listening to your body and to your tension zones, identifying mounting tension in its initial stages, and taking positive action to conquer your anxiety.

Conquering Performance Anxiety

The core of *The Mental Advantage* program is built upon proven relaxation, stress reduction, and visualization techniques applicable to equestrian sports. Targeted mental strategies include:

- **Relaxation** — Progressive Relaxation
  — Deep Breathing
- **Stress reduction** — Imagery & Your Calming Color
- **Visualization** — Positive Visualization

When individuals choose idealistic goals and do not attain them they typically feel badly, then chastise themselves for failing and for not working hard enough. This quickly evolves into a negative cycle which results in self-defeating behavior and increases performance anxiety. An obvious example of an idealistic goal is "I want to win every horse show.. . ." This goal seems extreme, yet some competitors feel defeated and a failure unless they take 1st place. You must accept that you cannot control everything. You have no control over show conditions, subjective opinions, bad weather, spooky occurrences, your horse's soundness, and a myriad of other factors. It's not enough to be good, you have to be lucky as well.

To develop a healthy perspective towards competition you must establish realistic goals. These goals will form the foundation of your mental practice program. Choose specific goals that you can control and realistically attain. For example, divide your goal to "succeed at horse shows" into more specific goals such as:

- To be relaxed prior and during your performance.
- To maintain correct riding posture . . . especially lengthening your legs, lowering your heels, and keeping your eyes forward, etc.
- To be precise in your seat and leg cues.
- To keep your horse straight and forward.

Here are some tips in forming realistic goals:

- Choose specific (and attainable) short term, mid term and long term goals, and write them down.
- State your goals only in positive terms such as "I will be calm . . . I can keep my heels down . . . I can remember my pattern . . ." etc.
- Visualize yourself successfully completing each step toward your goal.
- Consider time management: Have you allotted enough time to accomplish your goals?
- Gain useful insight into your goal development by asking for your trainer's input. What is his/her opinion on the goals you've established.
- Observe your peers at a similar level of preparation and expertise. Ask them how they reached that level of success.
- Keep a brief daily riding log. This will assist you in creating a more complete view of your goals and will help keep you focused on the facts and in touch with specific tasks.

Progressive Relaxation

Many equestrians are skilled at recognizing when tension is building in their horse, but lack the physical self-awareness to recognize tension in their own muscles. Developing sufficient self-awareness is a key step towards effective tension recognition, relaxation, and stress reduction. This progressive relaxation exercise will help you improve your body awareness, teach you to distinguish more clearly between states of physical tension and physical relaxation, and help you achieve a beneficial deep relaxation:

MA Exercise 1(a)

1. Make a fist and hold it as tight as you can while you count to 10. Relax your fist completely, letting it flop downward. Feel the difference of the sensations between tension and relaxation.

2. Make another fist and hold it with half as much tension as you did previously. Feel the difference between this fist and the first one. Note: There are different degrees of tension.

3. Now lie down on the floor, close your eyes, and fold your arms across your chest. Grasp your arms tightly for 10 seconds then relax. Again, feel the difference between tension and relaxation.

4. Experiment with your arms, face, stomach, legs, buttocks, etc. Hold each body part tightly for 10 seconds, then go completely limp for 30 seconds. Do this until you have progressed through your entire body.

An additional benefit of progressive relaxation is that it will help you learn which of your muscles are chronically tense. Remember that these muscles act as your tension zones and serve as initial stress signals.

Try this progressive relaxation exercise in the saddle before you begin your training or competitive performance:

MA Exercise 1(b)

1. Force your shoulders down and tightly tuck your chin into your chest. Hold for 10 seconds then relax for 30 seconds.

2. Force your shoulders down and tightly tuck your chin into your chest, then slowly lean forward. Hold for 10 seconds then relax. Concentrate on the difference between tension and relaxation. You should also feel increased suppleness and elasticity.

Breathing

Deep breathing is essential to all sport activities. The more oxygen you breathe into your respiratory system the better your performance will be. The opposite is also true: Breathing inadequate amounts of oxygen will hinder your performance. Shallow breathing, hyperventilation, and breath holding are all dysfunctional breathing habits and can cause fatigue, disorientation, and even injury. Deep breathing techniques will teach you how to breathe properly from deep in your lower chest and abdomen rather than in shallow breaths from your upper chest.

These techniques form the next step in enabling you to regain control over your own body and mind. This exercise will help you determine your present breathing pattern and develop a correct deep breathing technique:

- Lie down in a quiet place. Stretch out to full length and attempt to focus on your breathing location. Place your hand on your body where it rises and drops the most when you inhale and exhale. This is your breathing point.

- If your breathing point is in your upper chest, then you are breathing too shallow and you are not receiving enough oxygen to function efficiently. Your breathing point should evenly encompass both your chest and your abdomen. You want to feel your abdomen rise and fall at the same rate as your chest. This will deepen your breathing.

- Now try again. Breathe slowly through your nose, synchronizing your abdomen and chest to rise and fall at the same rate. As you inhale feel the air go all the way to the bottom of your lungs. Exhale gently.

- After you have developed a sense of your breathing, try this exercise while on your horse. See if your breathing changes when you are mounted.

Use your deep breathing technique to help yourself relax in this calming exercise:

MA Exercise 2

1. Stand using good posture. (You can also perform this exercise in the saddle.)

2. Breathe deeply and slowly through your nose, counting each breath: 1 - inhale, 2 - exhale, 3 - inhale, 4 - exhale . . . and so on.

3. Close your eyes and focus on counting your breaths. Around the 30th breath slowly open your eyes.

4. Try this 3 - 4 times a day.

5. If you are distracted by noise or by stray thoughts do not reproach yourself, simply return to counting your breaths. (Note: You can use this natural deep breathing technique to calm yourself virtually anywhere.)

Imagery & Your Calming Color

Many people can enhance their sense of security and relaxation through the use of imagery. Imagery simply is visualizing a pleasant scene and utilizing its calming effects. A highly effective imagery exercise is to envision your calming color. This exercise can be performed before your performance, your riding lesson, with your pre-competition program, or whenever you feel tense and insecure.

MA Exercise 3

1. Choose a color that creates a feeling of warmth, calmness, and security within you. Take a piece of paper and draw a square 2 inches across. Color your calming color inside the square. As you color try to experience the feelings your color brings to your senses.

2. Look into your color. Go ahead, squint your eyes and focus at it. Close your eyes and try to imagine your color. Try some deep breathing as you imagine your color.

3. Your color calms and soothes you. It makes you feel safe and warm. Try to imagine your calming color surrounding you and protecting you from all harm and negative energy.

Some people imagine that they are breathing their calming color in and it fills every pore of their body.

4. Each night as you lay in bed envision and feel your calming color and its soothing effects.

5. Once you are able to imagine your calming color quickly and consistently, perform this exercise every time you ride your horse.

Positive Visualization

Visualization can be defined as the innate ability to imagine yourself successfully or unsuccessfully completing an act. When used correctly, positive visualization can serve as mental support in the process of rapid problem solving. Visualization is not a new phenomenon. The American Indians have used visualization for hundreds of years as an important part of their culture.

Modern precedents exist as well. In 1972 an Australian psychologist, Alan Richardson, completed a study in visualization now recognized as a classic in sports psychology. Richardson divided a number of basketball players into 3 groups. For 20 days one group practiced making free throws, one group visualized making free throws, and the last group did neither. On the 21st day all 3 groups competed in a free throw contest. The results were surprising: The group of players who visualized making baskets easily compiled the best free throw shooting percentage and the highest score.

This study has since been replicated many times by other psychologists with the same

results: Visualization enhances skill. This does not suggest that visualization can replace the fundamentals of training. Visualization does not replace the experience itself. All of these basketball players had advanced basketball skills before they participated in the experiment. Mastery of the basic techniques and skills of your sport are necessary before visualization can be used effectively. Your best results will be attained by supplementing your training in the saddle with *The Mental Advantage* program, including positive visualization.

The practiced use of deep breathing, relaxation, and stress reduction will build a positive foundation by placing you in a receptive state of awareness and inner balance conducive to productive imagery. You must be in a relaxed state and be able to focus in a relaxed manner for visualization to be successful. No lasting benefits can be derived from any mental practice program until you are able to induce a true state of deep-relaxation.

Not everyone is successful with visualization and not everyone visualizes the same way. Some people "feel" visualization while others are auditory visualizers . . . they actually hear the rhythm of their horse's hoof beats instead of seeing it.

Here are a few tips for effective positive visualization:

- Visualize yourself being in complete control of your performance. Break down your performance into smaller, individual steps.

- Write down affirmations of the skill(s) you want to improve on. For example: "Keep my heels down, stay balanced and centered in the saddle, and keep my eyes up." This forms a written agreement with yourself that you can accomplish your specific goal(s). Symbolic visualization can assist you in your performance. If you are trying to prevent your chest from collapsing and your shoulders from rolling forward during the canter depart, then imagine your chest being pulled skyward by a string from the clouds and your shoulders being gently pushed back by a summer breeze.

- Use all of your senses when visualizing: Attempt to see, hear, touch, taste, and smell your images.

- Visualize in color instead of black and white . . . the more realistic your visualization, the better.

- Always end your visualization on a positive note. If you make an error, correct it before you conclude.

- Establish a regular visualization routine. Only through consistent practice will you become proficient at these techniques.

- You have worked on the details at home. You are prepared. Don't worry about every excruciating detail during your performance. Be confident and allow your visualization to work for you.

Try this positive visualization exercise:

MA Exercise 4

1. Choose any photo of you and your horse that you are proud of. It can be an action shot or a posed shot.

2. Find a quiet and calm place to perform your exercise.

3. Perform your progressive relaxation and deep breathing techniques to place yourself in a receptive state of mind.

4. Look at your photo with a "soft eye," that is keep your eyes slightly unfocused. Squinting slightly can help you maintain a "soft eye."

5. Close your eyes and imagine the photo in color and in as much detail as you can.

6. Acknowledge the good and successful qualities of you and your horse such as:

    "My horse has a beautiful neck and great conformation."

    "My horse is very athletic, and moves smoothly and gracefully."

    "We have a very balanced and collected canter."

    "I ride with good balance in the saddle."

7. Acknowledge your and your horse's triumphs. Allow yourself to be proud of your accomplishments.

For your visualization and imagery practice you should have someone videotape your training sessions and your competitive performances so you can observe your riding in private on your own television. Many horse shows have a professional video service taping the competition or you can enlist a friend. Initially, you may be uncomfortable watching yourself on a video and will be overly self-critical. It often takes several viewings before you can relax and enjoy the viewing. Once you can avoid extreme self-criticism, you are ready to begin using the video for productive visualization and imagery practice.

MA Exercise 5

1. Sit down in front of your VCR and television in a comfortable position. Relax using the deep breathing and imagery techniques detailed in MA Exercises 1-3. Begin with body tightening, follow with deep breathing, then imagine your calming color.

2. Begin viewing your video. Play your video in slow motion, if possible. This will give you better control over the imagery and visualization process.

3. View with a "soft eye," that is keep your eyes slightly unfocused as you watch your video. Squinting slightly can help you maintain a "soft eye."

4. Breathe slowly and rhythmically.

5. Concentrate on the positive aspects of your ride. Reward and affirm yourself on the good points of your ride.

6. Occasionally pause your VCR and visualize what you just saw. If that portion of your ride includes an error on your part, then close your eyes and visualize the correction. If you become distracted use your deep breathing and imagery techniques to help yourself become focused again.

7. Always end a visualization exercise on a positive performance and positive thoughts, never on a negative performance or with a self-critical negative thought.

It may take up to 7-8 visualization practice sessions before you become comfortable and proficient at the visualization-imagery process. The use of video will build your visualization skills and provide productive feedback which will aid your use of positive imagery during competition. If you do not have a good ride on video then get a copy of a successful professional ride and imagine yourself as the rider. Visualize yourself flowing in unison with the horse and executing a similar position in the saddle.

If you consistently practice your *Mental Advantage* program you will be able to better prepare for competition by visualizing a successful ride and being calm, confident, and aware. Visualize yourself successfully meeting your specific riding and competitive goals. (Staying balanced and centered in the saddle, maintaining good posture, cueing with precision, remembering your course pattern, and so on.) Envision yourself competing in a calm but assertive manner, and smoothly handling any problem you encounter.

The Mental Advantage During Competition

Here are some helpful tips for staying calm and focused during competition:

■ Maintain a consistent energy level by eating a high carbohydrate, low sugar, low fat diet and drinking plenty of water prior to and during the days you are competing.

■ Stretch thoroughly before you mount your horse.

- If necessary, tell critical family members to stay home (or simply away) the days you are competing.

- Use someone as a support system. This person should be a non-demanding friend whose knowledge and judgement you trust, such as your trainer.

- Take your time warming up your horse. Use a relaxation technique before your event. Don't wait until you feel tense. Listen to your tension signals.

- Visualize your ride before your enter the ring. Do not concentrate on the details, instead, *focus on the essence of a smooth ride.*

- When the competitor before you encounters a problem (falls to the ground, misses the correct lead, knocks a pole or rail down, etc.) do not become distracted. Remain completely focused on yourself , your horse, and your game plan.

- Ignore other competitors' negative emotions or comments. Use your relaxation techniques to construct a protective barrier around yourself and your horse.

- Your self-esteem is never dependent on winning. You are a good rider whether you win or not.

- Reward yourself and your horse on your improvements. Keep sight of your long term goals. Patience is invaluable.

- There will always be another horse show. A myriad of variable conditions exist that you cannot control . . . but you can choose to try again.

What if you experience an anxiety attack during your ride? How do you quickly salvage your ride and continue with your performance? If you have consistently practiced your mental program techniques then you are capable of implementing an emergency strategy for regaining control of your performance:

- Use your calming color/texture imagery and your deep breathing technique to regain control of your runaway negative thoughts.

- Then focus on the mechanics of your ride. Break down the remaining portion of your performance into simple individual steps such as maintaining good balance, concentrating on your horse's stride and pace and maintaining a good rhythm, executing your commands smoothly, maintaining correct posture, and so on.

To achieve full benefit you should practice all of the techniques in **The Mental Advantage** program twice a day for 3-4 weeks. Only through consistent practice and patience will you be able to use these natural calming methods when you need them the most. Mastery of the techniques in **The Mental Advantage** program will enable you to seize control of your mental and physical processes empowering you to perform with more confidence.

You will utilize your energy more productively and efficiently, and you will develop an improved awareness of yourself and your surroundings. You will learn to live more comfortably in the present. Reality exists only in the here and now . . . not in the past, nor in the future. When competing, you must exist in the present, so that you can concentrate fully on your horse, yourself, and your performance.

Your months of physical preparation and mental practice is working for you. Your horse is trained and prepared, and you are focused and relaxed. You can now instantly call upon proven calming strategies if you need them. You are capable of harnessing the power of positive visualization to enhance your performance. You are now ready to be tested and you welcome the competitive experience.

An anxious mind cannot exist within a relaxed body.

Edmund Jacobsen
the father of progressive relaxation

BUILDING A BALANCE BOARD

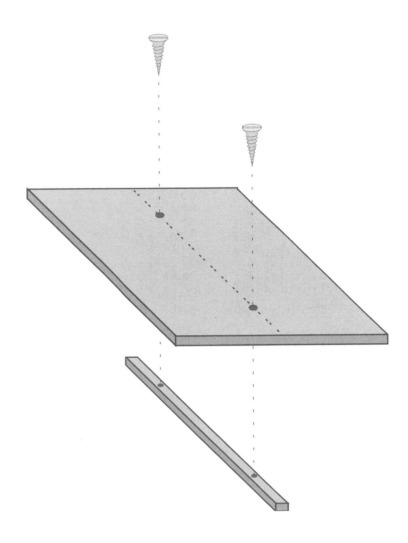

A balance board is easy to construct.
The supplies needed are:

- ❑ 1 - 1" x 12" x 16" board
- ❑ 1 - 2" x 2" x 15" board
- ❑ 2 - 1/4" x 2" wood screws
- ❑ wood glue
- ❑ pencil
- ❑ ruler or tape measure
- ❑ hammer
- ❑ screwdriver

- ❑ **Draw a line lengthwise down the middle of the board.**

- ❑ **Center two wood screws on the line and drive them through until they appear on the other side.**

- ❑ **Draw a line lengthwise down the middle of the 2" x 2", apply a bead of glue.**

- ❑ **Center the 2" x 2" on the 12" x 16" board and fasten tightly with the wood screws.**

- ❑ **Let it dry overnight before using.**

SUGGESTED READING

Centered Riding, Sally Swift, 1985, Trafalgar Square Farm, David & Charles Inc., North Pomfret, Vermont 05053, for info: St. Martin's/ Marek, 175 Fifth Avenue, New York, NY 10010.

Mental Toughness Training For Sports: Achieving Athletic Excellence, James E. Loehr, Ed.D., 1982, Forum Publishing Company, 1986 - The Stephen Greene Press, Inc., distributed by Viking Penguin Inc., 40 West 23rd Street, New York, NY 10010.

Nutrition Concepts & Controversies, Eva May Nunnelley Hamilton, Eleanor Noss Whitney, Frances Sienkiewicz Sizer, 1991, West Publishing Co., 50 West Kellogg Boulevard, St. Paul, MN 55164-0526.

Nutrition For The Athlete, Jennifer Anderson & Diane Preves, Colorado State University Cooperative Extension, No. 9.362.

Prescription for Nutritional Healing, James F. Balch, M.D., & Phyllis A. Balch, C.N.C, 1990, Avery Publishing Group Inc., Garden City Park, New York.

Principles of Athletic Training , 8th edition, Daniel D. Arnheim, D.P.E., A.T.C. & William E. Prentice, Ph.D., P.T., A.T.C., 1993, Mosby Year Book, 11830 Westline Industrial Drive, St. Louis, Missouri 63146.

Riding Out Of Your Mind, (video & booklet) Robert J. Rotella (director of sports psychology at the University of Virginia), Chrystine Jones (director of show jumping activities - U.S. Equestrian Team), Jean Sloanaker (University of Virginia), with USET Riders Leslie Burr and Peter Leone, 1984, Creative Media Group, Inc.

Sports Physiology, 3rd edition, Richard W. Bowers & Edward L. Fox, 1988, Wm. C. Brown Publishers, 2460 Kerper Boulevard, Dubuque, IA 52001.

Starting The Show Jumper, (video) Bill Robertson, 1987 Farnam Companies, Inc., P.O. Box 12068, Omaha, Nebraska 68112.

The Athlete's Guide To Sports Psychology: Mental Skills For Physical People, Dorothy B. Harris, Ph.D. & Bette L. Harris, Ed.D.,1984, Leisure Press, 597 Fifth Avenue, New York, NY 10017.

The Athletic Eye: Improved Sports Performance Though Visual Training , Dr. Arthur Seiderman & Steven Schneider, 1983, William Morrow & Company, Inc., 105 Madison Avenue, New York, NY 10016.

ACKNOWLEDGMENTS

I would like to thank each of the following for their valuable contributions to this book:

Jennifer Anderson, Ph.D., R.D. - nutrition extension specialist, Department of Food Science & Human Nutrition, Colorado State University.

Karen Bannister - APHA National Champion 1989, APHA World Champion 1990, APHA Reserve World All-Around 1991.

Barbara J. Beck, Ph.D. - health and fitness specialist & equestrian.

Katie Beck - 1990 Regional Saddleseat Equitation Champion, Top 20 - Saddleseat Equitation at 1991 U.S. Nationals, Top 20 - Ladies Sidesaddle at 1991 U.S. Nationals.

Cyndi Castiglioni - fitness instructor & illustration model.

Marliyn Colter - consultant.

Phyllis Dawson - USET member - highest placing American in 1988 Olympics in Seoul, Korea, (10th overall).

Terri Fithian - fitness instructor & illustration model.

Todd Gross - illustration model.

Troy Heikes - 1988, '89, '90 APHA National/World Reining Champion, 1990 APHA World Freestyle Reining Champion, 1990 APHA World Jumping Champion, 1990 APHA Superhorse, 1990 NHRA World Freestyle Reining Champion.

Barb Hermsen - certified fitness/conditioning instructor.

Debbie Horzepa - illustration model.

Ellene Busch-Kloepfer - dressage.

Margot Nacey, Ph.D. - licensed clinical psychologist, equine sports psychologist, & equestrian.

Tanya Nuhsbaum - fitness instructor, equestrian, & illustration model.

Anne Ricciardi - medical illustrator.

Bill Robertson - USET member 1962 & 1963, renowned show jumping instructor.

Kay Roth, Ph.D. - exercise physiologist.

Shawn Scholl, M.S. - exercise physiologist, fitness director, & competitive cyclist.

Barry Schneider - preliminary artist.

Charles Throckmorton - Colorado open jumping champion 1989, '90, '91.

Craig Vandegrift - certified fitness instructor, competitive bodybuilder.

Steve Wade, M.S. - physical therapist.

Mary Walhood. - dressage rider/instructor.